2005-2006

...and folklore

MayNe
ISLaNd

By V.A. Lindholm

Hidden Lighthouse Publishers
Canadian Rockies/Vancouver/Victoria

PuBLicatioN InFoRMatioN

Hidden Lighthouse Publishers
A division of Diskover Office Software Ltd.
575 Fernhill Rd
Site 3, Comp. 4
Mayne Island, BC V0N 2J0

Extreme care has been taken to ensure that all information presented in this book is accurate and up-to-date, and neither the author nor the publisher can be held responsible for any errors.

Cover design, page design and composition by Vicky Lindholm
All photos, with the exception of those listed under Credits, by Vicky Lindholm
Map by Vicky Lindholm

Front cover photo:
  Sunset on Mayne Island
Back cover photo:
  Campbell Bay, Mayne Island

To Lee for her advice,
encouragement and support, and
to Wendy for her great, Great
Blue Heron.

Contents

Contents

Introduction

When news of the discovery of gold on the Fraser River reached the outside world, Vancouver Island became the destination of gold miners on their way to the interior of British Columbia.[1] Waves and waves of eager miners advanced toward creeks proven to be extremely rich in gold. Where there was no route to the creeks, the miners entered the wilderness and traveled along the route they felt was best. As more and more men pressed north, trails gradually formed through the bush.[2]

It was in the summer of 1862 that the notorious killer, Boone Helm, stopped an Englishman, named Tom Collinson, on one of these trails. Helm aimed a shotgun at Tom's head, while his partner took Tom's six-shooter, and then cut the straps of his pack. They picked up Tom's pack and chased him down the trail at gunpoint, claiming his cash for their own, but missing a large amount of gold dust in his shirt pocket.[3]

William Tompkins Collinson was born in England, in the 1830's,[4] where he received only about five years of schooling[5]. He immigrated with his family to Canada in the 1850's, continuing on to Washington State where he heard the news of the Fraser River gold discoveries. He then spent some time mining for gold, reportedly helping to guide other miners over what was then called *Short Portage*, a place they had to carry their boat between two lakes.[6]

In the 1870's, Tom moved to Mayne Island with his Indian wife and their two children. Having pre-empted some land on the east side of Mayne, he homesteaded on what is now known as *Glenwood Farm*.[7] He later pre-empted land at *Miners Bay*, on the west side of Mayne.[8]

The ambitious Tom Collinson was an avid carpenter, having built several buildings on the bay at Mayne Island, including the first store.[9] In 1880, Tom became the first Postman on Mayne, operating the first post office from the home he had built there.[10] In the 1890's, he was made Justice of the Peace,[11] around the time that this was said about him:

> Tall, lean Mr. Collinson was the postmaster, and held the record for having the largest feet, and being the island's champion liar - or shall we say, Romantic. No matter what the topic of conversation, he could lie, and lie interestingly - as long as anyone would listen - about his experiences and utterly impossible exploits in that particular line, with a perfectly straight face, and then tell the same episode next time, with varying circumstances. It was a real gift!   Winifred Grey[12]

In the 1900's, a point on neighboring Galiano Island was named after Mr. Tom Collinson, **the Postman**. It is called *Collinson Point*.[13]

THINGS to KNOW

Just sit right back and you'll hear a tale…

Mayne is a relaxed island in the southern Gulf Islands. It lies in the rain shadow of the Vancouver Island Mountains, which protects it from storms that blow in from the Pacific Ocean. Often referred to as the *Banana Belt* of Canada, the Islands have a Mediterranean-type climate, which is warm during the day and cool at night.

Mayne Island enjoys an average of 2,000 hours of sunshine, annually. With the longest frost-free season in the country, spring begins as early as February. Because it rarely snows, a winter weekend on Mayne can be quite cozy with some logs on a *paia* (fire).

At only 7 km long and 4 km wide, Mayne is one of the smallest of the Gulf Islands. Its rolling hills and roads are reminiscent of an English *Illahee*

(countryside). There are no traffic lights, no curbs and no sidewalks, making it quite a quaint attraction.

Most of the Gulf Islands are uninhabited. However, at the time of this writing, Mayne had a population of about 900 permanent residents, a large percentage of which were over 55 years of age and retired.

Part-time residents own cottages as their 'home away from home', living as *weekenders* (people who spend weekends on Mayne) during the tourist season. At that time, the population swells to around 3,000.

MiNerS Bay

In the 1850's, no more than 500 people lived at the south end of Vancouver Island. However, when gold was discovered on the Fraser River, tens of thousands of *fifty-eighters* (miners living in the year 1858) came to British Columbia to seek their *tolla* (fortune).[14]

Miners in Victoria securing licenses for the gold rush in the mid-1800's, BC Archives A-04498

Since Mayne Island is located midway between Vancouver Island and the Fraser River, many of these gold miners began stopping overnight at the bay on the west side. That area of Mayne Island soon became known as *Miners Bay.*[15]

Miners Bay in the early 1900's, seen from the water, BC Archives A-09773

Today, Miners Bay is 'downtown' to Mayne Islanders, a seaside village where businesses and residents co-exist.

Miners Bay as it appears from the water today

Miners Bay Wharf

The first wharf to ever exist in the outer Gulf Islands was built at Miners Bay in the 1870's.[16] The wharf accommodated ships coming through the waterway that is officially called *Active Pass*, but was then known locally as *Plumper Pass*.[17]

Miners Bay wharf in the 1890's, the 2nd post office shown in the background, BC Archives C-03811

In the 1880's, the first wharf was replaced with a larger wharf that was twice as wide and extended an additional 15 m into the Pass.[18]

Miners Bay wharf in the 1930's, the post office shown in the background, BC Archives D-07435

In the 1930's, a circular bench was built at the foot of the wharf, to commemorate the coronation of King George VI. For several decades, Mayne Islanders gathered to socialize around the bench on *boat days* (when boats would dock at the wharf).[19]

Today, the bench still sits there, although the little tree that was planted in the center is just a bit larger now.

In the 1990's, the wharf at Miners Bay was destroyed by fire and a new wharf was built to replace it.[20]

Miners Bay wharf as it appears today

MayNe ISLaNd Post OFFice

To post their mail, residents initially rowed out into the Pass, intercepted the Hudson's Bay steamer ship and then handed their letters to one of the crew.[21]

In the 1880's, the Postmaster General approved a request for a post office on Mayne and a very prominent settler accepted the position as **the Postman**.

When a mail slot was cut into the side of his house on the bay, postal service began from there.[22]   His 1879 tax records indicate that the total tax paid for the property on which the post office sat was just 75 cents.[23]

In the 1890's, **the Postman** built a new home and store at the head of the new wharf, moving the post office to its second location.[24]

Initially, the address of the post office was simply *Plumper Pass*.[25] It was the first post office ever to serve the outer Gulf Islands.[26]   Steamer ships would first deliver the mail to neighboring Salt Spring Island.   Then, it would be delivered in a mailbag to Mayne. The mailbag was taken down to the boat on a wheelbarrow and was then exchanged for the bag from Salt Spring.[27] Postmen from neighboring Galiano, Pender and Saturna Islands would transport their mail, by rowboat, to and from Mayne.[28]

The S.S. Yosemite in the 1880's, BC Archives A-00299

S.S. Iroquois in the Gulf Islands in the early 1900's, BC Archives A-04780

The first building to serve as the *Mayne Island Post Office* was torn down in the 1970's. The second building still sits in front of the wharf on the bay. It operates as the *Springwater Lodge*.[29]

At the turn of the century, **the Postman** built a third building on the north side of the wharf, and moved his store and the post office there.[30] He then built

another building just north of it, which was operated as the *Mayne Store*.[31]

For decades, the post office operated from various stores at Miners Bay.[32] The building on the north side of the wharf changed owners many times and was torn down in the 1960's.[33] The Mayne Store is now a private residence on Georgina Point Road.

In the 1970's, the post office was moved to a building on Village Bay Road.[34] Today, that building operates as a hair salon and the post office sits in a storefront on Fernhill Road.

Mayne Island Museum

By the 1890's, smuggling and livestock rustling had become a big problem in the Gulf Islands. Because Mayne was centrally located and had a wharf at Miners Bay, a police constable was appointed there. The constable assumed law enforcement duties for all the islands. His police work was accomplished by rowboat.[35]

A few years later, the first *gaol* (jail) to exist in the outer Gulf Islands was built at Miners Bay. It was called the *Plumper Pass Lockup*.[36]

The *Plumper Pass Lockup,* in the 1950's, BC Archives B-07532

The Plumper Pass Lockup measured just 32 sq m, and contained a magistrate's court and two cells. The reinforced doors of the cells were locked with iron crossbars. The first prisoner to be held in one of the cells was arrested for larceny on Galiano Island.[37]

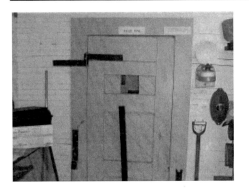

The *Plumper Pass Lockup* as it appears today

Shortly after the turn of the century, police headquarters were moved to Salt Spring Island.[38] At that time, constables on Pender Island became responsible for law enforcement on Mayne.[39]

In the 1970's, the jail was restored by the Mayne Island Agricultural Society, who converted it into the *Mayne Island Museum*.[40]

RCMP Station

Originally, the Gulf Islands were the responsibility of the British Royal Navy. However, with the influx of gold miners and settlers in the 1850's, the Provincial Police force was established to provide law and order in British Columbia.[41]

The BC Provincial Police sloop, *Mabelle*, at Mayne Island in the 1890's, BC Archives I-32839

One hundred years after it was established, the Provincial Police force was merged into the Royal Canadian Mounted Police.[42]

Today, there are over 6,000 *Queen's Cowboys* (RCMP) employed in British Columbia. However, on Mayne, where the crime rate is negligible and some people never lock their doors, there is still only one constable employed. The RCMP Station is located on Charter Road.

Mayne Island is not represented by a mayor or other town official. Its governing body is the Islands Trust. Established in the 1970's, the Trust is a unique federation of local island governments with a provincial mandate to make land use decisions that preserve and protect the southern Gulf Islands.[43]

MayNe IsLaNd AgricuLtuɾe HaLL

Around the turn of the century, a community hall was built at Miners Bay. It was originally called the *Maple Leaf Hall*. In the 1960's, it was officially renamed the *Mayne Island Agriculture Hall*,[44] but is known locally as the *Ag Hall*.

The site of many community events and markets, the Agriculture Hall and its fair grounds hosted its first fall fair in the 1920's.[45]

Today, the *Mayne Island Fall Fair* is the oldest fall fair in the outer Gulf Islands and continues to be a regular event at the fair grounds.[46] The fair grounds are also the site of the famous *Mayne Island Farmer's Market*.

In addition to the fall fair, the Agriculture Hall hosts the annual *Christmas Craft Fair*. It is also host to many civic functions, from performing arts presentations put on by the Mayne Island Concerts Society to musical concerts put on by the Mayne Island Little Theatre.

MaYNe ISLaNd CoMMUNity CeNter

Reportedly, a community hall once stood in the center of Mayne Island, but was destroyed by fire. A few years prior to this writing, a new *Mayne Island Community Activity Center* was built on Felix Jack Road to host civic functions.

ActiVe PaSS AuTo & MariNe

Until the introduction of gasoline-powered vehicles, boat was the only means of transportation to and from Mayne.[47] However, in the 1920's, automobiles began to appear.[48]

In the 1940's, a roadside gas pump was set up at Miners Bay. The oil and gas drums were transported from the Miners Bay wharf using man power. In the 1960's, a pump, with a pipeline that led to modern storage tanks, was installed. A few years later, a building was erected to enclose an automobile repair service.[49]

> **Treasure Hunt**
> *A well was built in the 1960's as a monument marking Canada's centennial celebration. Can you find it on Mayne Island?*

Today, you can gas up your *chikchik* (wagon) at the *Active Pass Auto and Marine* station, from what is still a single gas pump. The station also offers 24 hour towing and a two-bay garage. At the time of this writing, you could also obtain fishing licenses, tackle and bait there.

Miners Bay Trading Post

In the 1920's, a general store was built just east of the wharf at Miners Bay.[50] It changed owners several times until the 1950's, when it was run as a franchise called *Bambrick Stores Ltd.*[51]

Because there was no health centre on the island at the time, three rooms in the store were partitioned off to create a clinic for the doctors. This continued for many years.[52]

New owners changed the name of the store to *Hopkins Trading Post* in the 1960's. During much of the 1950's and 60's, the post office operated from this store. The name was then changed to *Mayne Island Trading Post*, but was soon changed again to *Miners Bay Trading Post*.[53]

In the 1970's, an apartment that had been built above the Miners Bay Trading Post caught fire. The fire spread to the store beneath it and a new building was erected to replace it.[54]

The Miners Bay Trading Post was the second business to be issued a liquor license in all of British Columbia.[55] Today, it functions as a grocery and liquor store.

Mayne Island Bank

The *Mayne Island Bank* clearly does not exist. However, at the time of this writing, there was an Automated Teller Machine (ATM) at the Miners Bay Trading Post, as well as at the Mayne Inn on Bennett Bay.

Mayne Street Mall

The *Mayne Street Mall* is a newer building that was built at Miners Bay to house local businesses.

At the time of this writing, the businesses in the Mayne Street Mall included realty and insurance offices, a grocery store and deli, as well as a bakery and café.

JapaNese MemoriaL GardeN

In the 1870's, the first Japanese to come to Canada were known as *Issei*. They settled on Vancouver Island where they encountered racism from the anti-Asian population of British Columbia, as well as from the government.[56]

Fishermen in the 1880's, believed to be the first Japanese in Victoria, BC Archives B-08405

In the early 1900's, the government denied the Japanese-Canadians the right to work in a profession, so when they came to Mayne, the first Japanese worked as laborers, cutting wood and making charcoal for the Fraser River canneries.[57]

Soon, Japanese-Canadian fishermen began settling on the southeast side of Mayne, at St. John Point and at what is now Horton Bay. Within their own community they knew Mayne Island as *Gon Island*.[58] Fortunately, they were well received by the Europeans who had already settled on Mayne.[59]

The Japanese-Canadian fisherman started concentrating on raising chickens. However, when freight increases made poultry farming unprofitable in the 1930's, many began to cultivate hothouse tomatoes and other vegetables, forming a successful marketing cooperative called *Active Pass Growers Association*.[60] The cooperative boasted almost 35,000 sq m of greenhouses, made from glass imported from Japan.[61]

Label used by the Active Pass Growers Association in the 1930's

By the 1940's, the Japanese-Canadian community comprised one-third of Mayne's population. However, when the Japanese attacked Pearl Harbor, the Japanese-Canadians were taken from their homes on Mayne and were dispatched to the interior of British Columbia where internment camps had been set up in remote towns.[62]

At the same time, the Canadian Navy impounded all Japanese-Canadian fishing boats that existed in British Columbian waters.[63] Some of the European settlers looked after the remainder of their property until the activity was made illegal and was punishable by jail time.[64]

Japanese-Canadian internment camp, south of Slocan City, in the 1940's, BC Archives I-60959

After World War II, the property belonging to the Japanese-Canadians was sold off by government agents acting on orders made under the provisions of the War Measures Act. Their property was often sold to war veterans.

Post-internment, the Japanese-Canadian families were still prohibited from returning to the British Columbian coast. They were only allowed to return to Japan or to travel east of the Rocky Mountains. Many traveled to the neighboring province of Alberta, to work as laborers on sugar beet farms.[65]

Eventually, the right to vote was returned to the Japanese-Canadians.

However, very few of them ever returned to Mayne to receive that right.

The *Japanese Memorial Garden* is a development that was completed only a few years prior to this writing. Built by Mayne Islanders, on what was once a Japanese-Canadian fruit farm,[66] this heritage park was undertaken to commemorate the Japanese-Canadians who originally settled and worked on Mayne.

The garden of Katsura trees, Japanese cherries, flowering plums and rhododendrons surrounds a large pond.

The Japanese Garden is visited by tourists during the summer and is decorated with an impressive display of festive lights during the Christmas season. It is located at Dinner Bay Community Park, which can be accessed by way of Williams Place.

MayNe IsLaNd SchooL

In the 1880's, a prominent Mayne settler donated some property in the center of Mayne Island for the site of a school. With **the Postman** also active in arranging for it,[67] a schoolhouse was built. It measured just 40 sq m and contained only one classroom.[68]

When classes began, the enrollment numbered 20 children, which increased to 30 children a year later.[69] The children who attended the school came not only from Mayne, but also from Galiano and Saturna Islands.[70]

In the 1890's, a second, larger school was built. Because there was no indoor plumbing, the daily drinking water was carried uphill from a well. To heat the schoolhouse, a student was paid to light the stove an hour before the morning classes.[71]

Second schoolhouse, 1890's, MIVF Archives

When the Japanese-Canadians were taken from their homes at the start of World War II, 17 school children were evacuated. With only four children left in attendance at the school, it was closed for two years.[72] In the 1960's, it was closed permanently and moved to Felix Jack Road.[73] It now functions as the social hall for the Mayne Island Volunteer Firefighters Association.

Second schoolhouse as it appears today

In the 1950's, a third, one-room school was built where the first school had been built. Since then, it has had many additions built around it.[74]

When the gymnasium was added to the new school in the 1970's, students collected items that represented current events and inserted them into a 'time capsule'. They buried the capsule beside the gymnasium door. A few years prior to this writing, a student from Galiano Island was chosen to dig up the capsule and open it to reveal its contents.[75]

Today, the new *Mayne Island School* functions as an elementary and junior secondary school, serving the children of Mayne, Galiano and Saturna Islands. It accommodates about 65 full-time equivalent students, offering programs from kindergarten to grade 11. Grade 12 students are transported to schools on neighboring islands by the *Scholar Ship* (a water taxi that carries school children).

Mayne Island Fire Department

Because fires had destroyed so many buildings on Mayne Island in the first half of the century, it was incorporated into a fire protection district in the 1960's.[76]

Unfortunately, the Agriculture Hall, which functioned as the fire hall, was made out of wood, and the only fire protection available was a forestry pump and several hundred feet of hose.[77]

Within two years, a tanker truck was purchased for one dollar, followed by the purchase of an 800-gallon truck. When the *Mayne Island Volunteer Fire Brigade*, along with a *high muckymuck* (fire chief), began to meet regularly for fire drills, the brigade moved to a three bay hall on Felix Jack Road.[78]

In the 1970's, a modern, fire pumper truck was purchased and an electronic, fire alarm system was installed.[79]

Today, the *Mayne Island Fire Department* consists of in excess of 20 *smoke eaters* (fire fighters). By their own admission, they "willingly rush toward a burning building that everyone else is rushing away from".

Mayne Island Health Center

A few of the settlers' wives were well known for their skills in midwifery. Many of the women from the other islands would board with them when they had their children.[80]

In the 1920's, a retired Royal Canadian Northwest Mounted Police surgeon became one of the first resident doctors on Mayne.[81] He set up his practice in a building jutting out over Miners Bay.[82] Today, the building is a private residence on Georgina Point Road and can be seen from the wharf.

In the 1930's, another doctor set up his practice in a small building that sat behind the lodge at the wharf. It was simply called, *Surgery*.[83] Today, the owners of the Springwater Lodge use the building for storage.

> **Treasure Hunt**
> *There is a piece of stained glass depicting a settler and his oar with a ship in the background. Can you find it on Mayne Island?*

In the 1960's, a first aid station was built across from the school. At around the same time, an ambulance was purchased and a volunteer crew was appointed to operate it.[84]

A decade later, the *Mayne Island Health Center* was opened on Felix Jack Road. An ambulance station was also established there.[85]

In the 1990's, the *Ron Mitchell Memorial Heliport* was dedicated to Mayne Island. It serves as a landing area for helicopters transporting patients to major hospitals on Vancouver Island, as well as to the mainland.

Today, a resident physician and a visiting public health nurse provide health care to Mayne Islanders from the Mayne Island Health Center. The center also employs other health care workers, such as a massage therapist, physiotherapist, chiropractor and dentist.

MoNtroSe FerNHiLL BuSiNeSS Area

The *Montrose Fernhill Business Area* is located at the corner of Montrose Road and Fernhill Road. It was established

as one of only two business sections on Mayne.[86]

The Fernhill Centre operates as a commercial mall in the area. At the time of this writing, the businesses in the mall included art galleries and a cafe.

A gift store, called Hidden Lighthouse Gifts and Essentials, operates as a home-based business in the area. It provides the local Islanders with essentials, and provides visitors with a variety of gifts and collectibles.

Fırst Natıons Reserve

First Nations people lived in the Gulf Islands long before the Europeans arrived 200 years ago. They were known as the *Coast Salish*, and were members of the *Nanaimo*, *Chemainus*, *Cowichan*, *Saanich* and *Songhees* tribes. The five tribes spoke the languages of *Halq'emeylem* and *Lekungenung.*[87] They knew Mayne Island as *Sqthaq.*[88]

Current opinion holds that a trade language was eventually developed for communication between the European fur traders and First Nations people. This language evolved into *Chinook Jargon*, with some words making their way into modern-day, British Columbian English.[89]

First Nations settlement on Helen Point, Mayne Island, Royal BC Museum PN-5734

In the 1850's, it was the responsibility of the Governor of the Colony of Vancouver Island to negotiate with the leaders of the First Nations regarding the right to occupy their land. However, when some of the Indians in the Gulf Islands would migrate to the Fraser River during the summer, the British would simply take their land.[90]

In the 1860's, a settler from Washington State decided to join a Mayne Islander in working the land he owned at Miners Bay. On an Easter weekend, the settler set out to move his family to Mayne in two boats. When they encountered a storm, one of the boats, carrying only the settler and one of his daughters, took shelter on Saturna Island.[91]

As they sat by a fire, the settler was shot in the back. His daughter ran, but was caught and stabbed to death.[92]

Shortly thereafter, two other settlers were shot on Pender Island. One of the settlers died of his wounds, but the other lived to describe his attackers as Indian.[93]

When the British learned of the attacks, they sailed their gunboat, the HMS *Forward*, to Miner's Bay. They took a half-breed Indian from Mayne aboard their boat to be their interpreter. He guided them to where they could survey the sites of the attacks.[94]

The result of their surveys prompted the British to sail north, to Kuper Island, where a Coast Salish group of Indians, called *Lamalcha*, lived. There, they anchored their gunboat in the bay in front of the Lamalcha village.[95]

Unknown to the British, Lamalcha warriors were hiding on both sides of the bay when they arrived. When the British fired, the warriors returned their fire and a 16-year-old sailor was killed. He was the first and last British serviceman killed in action in British Columbia.[96]

After several hours, the British attack proved futile. Defeated, they pulled their boat out of the bay. It was the only tactical defeat ever inflicted by a tribal group over the British Royal Navy.[97]

HMS *Forward*, 1860's, BC Archives B-00268

It is estimated that the Lamalcha Indians numbered just over 100 people, most of which were children. In spite of this, it took two additional expeditions by the British, with three ships and 500 men, to overtake them. These expeditions occurred from various locations in the Gulf Islands, including Galiano Island. The battle was one of the largest military operations in British Columbia's history.[98]

The Lamalcha village was then burned and later confiscated. Seven natives were captured, tried and executed for the murders on Saturna and Pender Islands. The Lamalcha war chief was never captured.[99] A point on Saturna Island was later named after the settler and his daughter who were killed there. It is called *Murder Point*.[100]

Bad Water and Bad Indians

Storms, currents and reefs made this area the most hazardous of the Pacific Coast; Indians were last on the list of dangers. Then they became first, and the Royal Navy was in for a full-fledged war . . .

By T. W. PATERSON

Photos Courtesy Author

SAVAGE STORMS, treacherous currents and hidden reefs took a heavy

toll of mariners plying British Columbia's "Graveyard of the Pacific" 100 years ago. But the greatest danger to seaman and settler alike was the unpredictable Indians who lived along the rocky, beautiful shoreline.

Probably the first victim of Indian attack in the Pacific Northwest was a

HMS Forward (below) fought hostile Indians for almost ten years.

Courtesy British Columbia Provincial Archives

Article about the attack on the Lamalcha in the 1860's, Frontier Times, March 1972

This colonial war paved the way for the alienation of Indian land on eastern Vancouver Island and the Gulf Islands, without mutual agreement. It is a war that has been largely ignored by historians and does not appear in most general histories of British Columbia.[101]

By the late 1860's, the British had given up trying to negotiate with the Indians and implemented an ad hoc system of creating reserves within the confines of lands already claimed by settlers in the pre-emption system.[102]

A decade later, First Nations was allotted a 1.3 sq km reserve on Helen Point, on the west side of Mayne Island.[103]

Helen Point seen from Galiano Island, Salt Spring Archives M-002

In the 1950's, when the Saanich Tribe was divided into five bands, the *Tsartlip Band* was created.[104]

A few years prior to this writing, the Tsartlip Band began plans to log a portion of Helen Point. When news of the planned logging became general knowledge, opposition arose.[105] However, when the logging was complete, the Tsartlip were presented with an award by Tourism Victoria, as a testimonial to the intelligent stewardship they showed during the process.[106]

The reserve on Helen Point is still owned by the Tsartlip Band today, but is occupied by members of the Cowichan Tribe.[107]

Helen Point contains the oldest, recorded, human settlement remains in the southern Gulf Islands.[108]

Helen Point in the 1940's, BC Archives I-20664

Helen Point as it appears today

PLaceS to Stay

Mayne Island was one of the earliest summer resorts to ever exist on the West Coast of Canada.[109] A surprising number of accommodations date back to the early 1900's when it became an important Pacific Northwest resort island. At that time, the 100 or so residents rapidly began to develop tourist facilities to capitalize on their island's growing popularity.

The magnificent Point Comfort Hotel overlooking Maude Bay in the early 1900's, BC Archives E-07867

Today, you can see some good examples of turn-of-the-century Victorian architecture around Mayne, particularly at Miners Bay. Some of the inns and lodges are still in operation and, along with some other accommodations, have been listed in this book.

A CoachHoUSe oN OySter Bay B&B

A Coachhouse on Oyster Bay Bed & Breakfast is a year-round B&B. It is located on Bayview Drive, overlooking one of the preferred kayak launching points. Phone (250) 539-3122

Active Pass B&B

The *Active Pass Bed & Breakfast* is located at Miners Bay. Guided salmon fishing charters are also provided. Phone (250) 539-5034

Bayview B&B

The *Bayview Bed & Breakfast* is a seasonal B&B located on Steward Drive. Bicycles and other recreational equipment are available. Guests can use the dock at Horton Bay for boat launching. Phone (250) 539-2924

Blue Vista Resort

The *Blue Vista Resort* is a year-round, cottage resort located on Arbutus Drive. The resort is a short distance from two launching and landing sites on Bennett Bay. Kayak and bike rentals are available. Phone 1-877-535-2424

Coastal Escapes

Coastal Escapes is an oceanfront cottage rental on Dinner Point, on the southwest side of Mayne. It provides for two vacation homes. Phone 1-866-829-9312

Fernhollow Campground

The *Fernhollow Campground* contains a unique, self-contained, cob cottage rental made from a mixture of sand, clay and straw.

Campsites are also available at the campground. The campgrounds are located on Horton Bay Road. No reservations are required. Phone (250) 539-5253

Mayne Inn

In the early 1900's, a French company began construction of a plant at Bennett Bay, on the east side of the island. The plant included a large wharf extending into the bay. A boarding house was also built to accommodate the workers.[110]

At the onset of World War I, the plant was closed, without ever becoming operational. The Tudor-style boarding house remained empty until the 1940's, when it was converted into a hotel called *Hollandia Hotel*. In the 1950's, the name was changed to *Arbutus Lodge* and then to *Mayne Inn*, in the 1960's.[111]

In the 1970's, the owners of the Mayne Inn attempted to build a large, commercial dock, adjacent to one of the best bathing beaches on Mayne. The project was estimated to cost as much as \$60,000. However, before they received the necessary re-zoning, they started work on the dock. With half of the project completed, they were ordered to stop and begin its demolition.[112]

Today, the Mayne Inn, on Arbutus Drive, is operated by new owners. Phone (250) 539-3122

Mayne Island Eco Camping

The *Mayne Island Eco-Camping* campground is located on Maple Drive. A kayak and boat launch are available. Phone (250) 539-2667

Oceanwood Country Inn

In the 1980's, a family purchased a large Tudor house on Dinner Bay Road, overlooking the channel near Dinner Bay. They transformed the house into the *Oceanwood Country Inn*. The Inn is still operational today. Phone (250) 539-5074

Root Seller Inn

At the turn of the century, a Victorian style home was built in the heart of Miners Bay. It was later developed into the *Root Seller Inn*. Today, the Root Seller Inn is one of Mayne Island's oldest Inns. It is also the home of a bookstore. Phone (250) 539-2621

Seal Beach Cottage

The *Seal Beach Cottage* is located on Maple Drive, overlooking Miners Bay. Boat moorage and launch is available. Phone (250) 539-2667

Seal Reef Cottages

The *Seal Reef Cottages* include three cottages situated in separate locations on Mayne. Head office is located on Edith Point Road. Phone (250) 539-9902

Springwater Lodge

In the 1890's, after his eldest children had left home, **the Postman** turned the two-story house he had built by the wharf into a boarding house. He ran the boarding house for about 15 years, in an effort to supplement his income.[113]

The Springwater Lodge, BC Archives C-03811

After the turn of the century, **the Postman's** daughter took over the operation of his boarding house, renaming it *Grandview Lodge*.[114]

The Springwater Lodge in the early 1920's, BC Archives B-03269

Soon, the Grandview Lodge had a false front and a six bedroom wing off the side. By the 1930's, the lodge had developed such a good reputation that the owners were able to add indoor plumbing, electric lights and a walk-in refrigerator, in spite of the economic depression of that decade. They charged $14 for a single room, meals included.[115]

In the 1960's, new owners changed the name to *Springwater Lodge*.[116] Reportedly, a '67 Volkswagen van was impounded on Mayne after it crashed into the lodge. The owner who pressed charges was irate and unclothed.

Today, the Springwater Lodge is reputed to be the oldest, continuously operating hotel in all of British Columbia. Parts of the original home still remain.[117] Phone (250) 539-5521

The Springwater, 1930's, BC Archives D-07435

The Springwater Lodge as it appears today

TiNKerer's B&B

In the 1880's, an early Mayne settler built a small store and a hotel overlooking Miners Bay. He named the hotel, *Mayne Island House*, but it was known locally as *Robson's Hotel*. When it was expanded by new owners, it was renamed *Mayne Island Hotel*.[118]

In the 1920's, the hotel was destroyed by fire[119] and a new house was built on the site. In the 1980's, a trained toolmaker and his wife renovated and restored the house, calling it *Tinkerer's Retreat*. The retreat served them as their summer home, and bed and breakfast.[120]

Today, the *Tinkerer's Bed and Breakfast*, on Sunset Place, still functions as their summer home. They also use it to run a tool sharpening business, sharpening tools the old-fashioned way. Phone (250) 539-2280

THiS Mad Tapestry Studio & Retreat

This *Mad Tapestry Studio and Retreat* is a B&B overlooking the channel near Dinner Bay. Phone (250) 539-3699

WiNe & RoSeS ViLLa

The *Wine and Roses Villa* is a B&B located on Minty Drive, at Miners Bay. Phone (250) 539-9997

WayS to Get ArouNd

Before the turn of the century, visitors would often be transferred from their ship to Mayne Island, by **the Postman** who would row them to shore. They would see his large hands reaching up to them as they climbed down their ship's ladder to his waiting rowboat.[121]

Early Mayne Island settlers traveled everywhere by rowboat. Some used to row to Vancouver Island and then take a *latleh* (train) to Victoria. Others rowed to *Big Smoke* (Vancouver). Often, they held rowing competitions between Mayne and Galiano Island, across the Pass.[122]

Early settlers in a rowing competition across Active Pass, Salt Spring Archives G-66

Today, Mayne is one of the prime areas for kayaking in the Gulf Islands. It provides easy access to some hot kayaking spots around Georgeson Island and the Belle Chain Islets to the east. They are highly valued as seal and sea lion haulouts, as well as nesting sites for several species of birds.

Late summer and fall is the best time to kayak around Mayne because of morning and evening calms. You can also travel by *stinkpot* (motorboat) or by sailboat.

If you choose to boat in Active Pass, keep in mind that it is just that – active! All ferry traffic between Vancouver Island and the mainland travels through this 5.5 km pass, making it one of the busiest bodies of water on the entire West Coast. Near-collisions between ferries and sport fishermen have occurred in the Pass, the most dangerous area being around Helen Point.

When boating around Mayne, it is important to listen for the ships' horns. If you hear five short blasts, someone's boat is on a collision course with the ship.

Mayne can be an enjoyable island to cycle, so another way to get around is by bicycle or scooter. Cyclists can tour the entire island in a day, even with stops at its bays. However, some areas, such up Hall Hill on Georgina Point Road, are rather difficult. The easiest ride is down Fernhill Road to Bennett Bay.

Keep in mind that there are no shoulders on the roads and, although some appear to be there for casual country driving, many of them are major thoroughfares that the Islanders use to conduct their business.

ISLaNd CHarters

Island Charters offers full and half-day sailing trips in a 10 m offshore sailboat. Phone (250) 539-5040

BLUe VISta KayaKING aNd BIKe ReNtaLS

Blue Vista Kayaking and Bike Rentals provides day and evening interpretive kayak tours. Professional instruction is also provided. Used kayaks can be purchased. Bike rentals are also available. Phone 1-877-535-2424

Mayne Island Eco Camping Tours & Charters

Mayne Island Eco-Camping Tours and Charters provides kayak and boat tours. Kayaks and canoes can also be rented. Instruction is available. Phone (250) 539-2667

Mayne Island Kayak, Canoe and Bike Rentals

Mayne Island Kayak, Canoe & Bike Rentals provides kayak rentals and guided tours. Instruction is included. Bike rentals are also available. Phone (250) 539-5599

Gulf Islands Water Taxi

Operating from Salt Spring Island, *Gulf Islands Water Taxi* provides scheduled trips between Miners Bay and Salt Spring Island. Phone (250) 537-2510

M.I.D.A.S. Taxi

If you need to get somewhere quickly, and you do not have your own *island beater* (old car parked on Mayne), you can hail the *MIDAS Taxi* (Mayne Island Drive And Service)). It will take you to and from the ferry, as well as around Mayne. Phone (250) 539-3132

Seair Sea Planes

Seair Sea Planes offers daily, scheduled, float plane flights between the Vancouver Airport and Miners Bay. Phone 1-800-44SEAIR

Mayne Island Scooter Rentals

Mayne Island Scooter Rentals provides scooters for touring around Mayne. Phone (250) 539-2929

THiNgS to See

Mayne Island is a relaxing getaway with many areas to wander about. Many people come to Mayne simply to stroll out to the lighthouse, gaze at the Victorian architecture, or go for a drive in the country.

There are four major routes on Mayne. *Fernhill Road* runs east and west, bisecting the island. Village Bay Road connects Fernhill Road to the ferry terminal and to the south end of the island. Georgina Point Road turns into Waugh Road and then into Campbell Bay Road, circumventing the north end of the island. Horton Bay Road splits off at Gallagher Bay Road, which turns into Mariners Way, connecting several minor roads along the south end of the island.

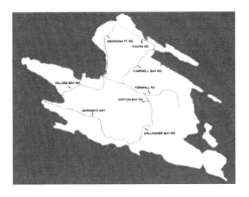

Active Pass Light Station

In the 18th century, the British began surveying the West Coast. During one of their voyages, they landed on a point in the Pass. One hundred years later, **the Postman** discovered a British one cent coin that had been lost on that point.[123] It was dated 1784.[124]

Around that time, in the 1880's, construction of the *Active Pass Light Station* began on that same point.[125] The lighthouse at the station was called the *Plumper Pass Lighthouse*.[126]

By the early 1900's, freighters from all over the world were coming through the Pass and the lighthouse kept the traffic at the entrance to the Pass away from the rocks on the point.

The resident who took the position of lighthouse keeper lived in the lighthouse with his family, providing service for over 35 years.[127]

Initially, an ordinary oil lamp provided the light. Each night, the lighthouse keeper lit the lamp at sundown and blew it out at sunrise.[128] If the machinery operating the fog bell malfunctioned, he would ring the bell by hand whenever a steamer entered the Pass.[129]

Georgina Point Lighthouse in the late 1800's, BC Archives A-04588

The light station that exists today was built in the 1940's.[130] Because the point, itself, had officially been named *Georgina Point*,[131] the lighthouse was renamed the *Georgina Point Lighthouse*.[132] One of the original buildings was then moved to another location, where it now functions as a house on an organic farm.

Georgina Point Lighthouse in the 1950's, BC Archives I-21115

In the 1960's, the beacon tower was built at the light station.[133] A decade later, a communication tower was built in Mount Parke Regional Park, as part of a navigational radar system for aiding the local shipping traffic.[134] It can be seen from ferries arriving at Village Bay.

The Georgina Point Lighthouse can be seen from the ferries crossing Georgia Strait, the waterway on the north side of Mayne. In the 1980's, it celebrated its centennial, a distinction held by only a few lighthouses on the entire West Coast.

The tower, which is owned by the Canadian Coast Guard, was de-staffed in the 1990's and is now closed. However, the Active Pass Light Station, which sits on park grounds, is still open to the public. It is accessible from Georgina Point Road.

Georgina Point Lighthouse as it appears today

THe ANCHOrage

In the early 1900's, a prominent settler established Mayne's first hothouse industry. He pioneered the use of double-trussed greenhouses, which he built on Georgina Point.[135]

In his greenhouse operation, he grew some of the first hothouse tomatoes in the province. However, in spite of the fact that he employed Chinese workers for 20 years, he never learned one word of the Chinese language.[136]

In the 1920's, he built a larger operation at Miners Bay, where he specialized in flowers and tomatoes. He called it *Mayne Island Nurseries*. At 90 m long and 12 m wide, his greenhouse was the largest in all of British Columbia.[137]

Eventually, the settler's hothouse industry became so large that his weekly shipments would often delay the steamer ships at the wharf for hours. As a result, he became well known on the West Coast as 'The Tomato King'.[138]

Greenhouses near Miners Bay in the 1940's, BC Archives D-07434

The successful settler suffered in the Stock Market crash of the 1920's and, subsequently, retired in the 1930's. When the Japanese took over his tomato industry, he began catering to guests from his home overlooking the bay. He called his guesthouse *The Anchorage.*[139]

In the 1950's, the settler ceased operating The Anchorage as a guesthouse.[140] Today, a descendant resides in the home, which is located on Georgina Point Road. Reportedly, the hill on which The Anchorage was built was named after the settler. The field further up that hill is all that remains of Mayne Island Nurseries.

St. Mary Magdalene Church

In the 1890's, the *St. Mary Magdalene Anglican Church* was built on Georgina Point Road. It was the first church to serve the outer Gulf Islands.[141]

A few years after the church was built, a uniquely shaped, 400-pound, piece of sandstone was discovered on the shore of Saturna Island. The Vicar, who was the founder of the church, transported it by rowboat, so it could be used as the baptismal vessel.[142]

In the early 1900's, a fire broke out on the church grounds and the building

where the Vicar had taken up residence was destroyed. Fortunately, the church, itself, was saved by its parishioners and was able to accommodate an adjoining cemetery a decade later.[143]

St. Mary Magdalene Anglican Church in the 1890's, BC Archives G-01421

In the 1950's, the Royal Canadian Legion erected a *lych* gate in memory of the men who died in the World Wars.[144] It provides for a traditional, English, church yard entrance where wonderful examples of Arbutus trees grow.

St. Mary Magdalene Anglican Church as it appears today

In the 1980's, the church held its first fair, which continues to be a regular event on the church grounds each summer.[145]

A decade later, another fire ravaged through the forest behind the church. Reportedly, it loosened large boulders and sent them down into the church grounds where they now form part of a Centennial Memorial Garden.

MeadoWMist FarM

Meadowmist Farm sits in a large valley at Village Bay. In the 1980's, the farm began raising animals to be used for food and other products, such as soap, quilts and clothing. Today, the farm also raises a novelty bird from Chile, called the *Araucana*, which lays green eggs.[146] Since the farm occasionally raises pigs as well, you might want to purchase some Araucana eggs so you can cook up some green eggs and ham.

Today, the church, itself, is still very much the way it was at the turn of the century.

Meadowmist Farm products can be purchased at the farm, as well as in Mayne's grocery stores. The farm is accessible by way of Mariner's Way. People are encouraged to visit. The contribution is one *tooney* (two Canadian dollars) per person. Phone (250) 539-3316

Treasure Hunt

In the 1980's, an Irish settler built the St. Francis of Assisi Memorial Chapel. Can you find it on Mayne Island?

GLeNWOOd

In the 1860's, a prominent Mayne settler emigrated from England to Vancouver Island, at the age of 14. When he found prospecting for gold too difficult, he set sail for the Gulf Islands and landed in Horton Bay, on Mayne.[147]

As he explored the area around what is now Horton Bay Road, he located a valley in which he started growing crops and built his first log home. He called the farm *Glenwood*, eventually

developing it into a highly successful, dairy farm.[148]

In the 1870's, the young settler formed a partnership with the man who would later become **the Postman**.[149]

Soon, it became a tradition for the children attending the Mayne Island School to picnic at Glenwood Farm, to celebrate the end of each school year.[150]

Today, Glenwood Farm is the oldest farm on Mayne and is one of the largest of the old homesteads in all of the Gulf Islands.[151] Although one of the first houses on the farm was destroyed by fire,[152] at the time of this writing, a descendant who lived in the third house to be built on the farm was still working it.[153]

A monument commemorating the farm and the descendant of its first settler exists on Horton Bay Road.

Cob Homes

Cob homes are made from a mixture of sand, clay and straw. The mixture is wet enough to mold, yet dry enough to build up without forms. There are a few cob homes on Mayne Island. Reportedly, one of the homes is the first code-approved cob house ever to exist in Canada.

The cob home on Georgina Point Road is called *The Hobbit House*. It was made using the same method used for making cob houses in England and Wales, in the 15th and 16th century. There are also cob homes on Horton Bay Road. Tours of some of the cob homes are available. Email pat@cobworks.com.

Treasure Hunt
A parking sign reads, "Thou Shalt Not Park Here". Can you find it on Mayne Islands?

Valhalla Gardens

Valhalla Gardens is a wonderful flower garden that thrives among a forest of giant Western Red Cedar and Douglas-Fir. A few years prior to this writing, the gardens hosted the first *FestivaLavender* event, which continues

to be an annual event. The gardens are located on Village Bay Road.

Places to Eat

Before the turn of the century, there were already two hotels on Mayne; the *Mayne Island House* at Miners Bay and a three storey, 30-room hotel, called *Point Comfort*, on what is now Georgina Point.

Because there were no other saloons in operation in the outer Gulf Islands, Mayne was known as *Little Hell* to the people of the neighboring islands. This distinction continued until Prohibition in the 1920's.[154]

Whatever you hunger or thirst for, there are some good restaurants on Mayne Island today where you can get great *muckamuck* (food) and drink.

Mayne Inn

The historic *Mayne Inn*, on Arbutus Drive, offers an assorted menu of Pacific Northwest cuisine, with emphasis on locally grown and harvested Gulf Island products. Phone (250) 539-3122

Mayne Mast

In the 1920's, a Japanese fisherman purchased a turn-of-the-century, Victorian style home at Miners Bay.[155]

Later, his family purchased a small greenhouse, which they dismantled and moved, piece by piece, to Miners Bay. After re-assembling the greenhouse alongside his home, the fisherman began to use it to grow hothouse tomatoes.[156] He became successful in this venture and developed a tomato growers cooperative on Mayne.[157]

In the 1930's, the Japanese-Canadian enlarged his home, only to have his family evacuated from it at the start of World War II.[158]

In the 1970's, the home was converted into a restaurant called the *Five Roosters Restaurant*.[159]

Today, the restaurant, located on Village Bay Road, operates as the *Mayne Mast*. It offers breakfast, lunch and dinner. At the time of this writing, you could also find a variety of garden gnomes for sale there.

Oceanwood Country Inn

The *Oceanwood Country Inn*, on Dinner Bay Road, features gourmet, West Coast cuisine and wines. The four-course dinner menu changes nightly. Reservations are required. Phone (250) 539-5074

Springwater Lodge

The *Springwater Lodge*, at Miners Bay, offers breakfast, lunch and dinner. Dinner reservations are highly recommended. Phone (250) 539-5521

Sunny Mayne Bakery Café

Breakfast is served from 7 am at the *Sunny Mayne Bakery Café*, located in the Mayne Street Mall at Miners Bay. There are also lunch specials. Phone (250) 539-2323

Places to Shop

Vancouver Island was first occupied by the Hudson's Bay Company, whose employees had settled there in the 1840's and laid the foundation for what became an important trading station.[160]

At the turn of the century, **the Postman** would row out to the steamer ships from the Hudson's Bay, Spencer's and Woodwards, and would return with parcels in his rowboat.[161]

Today, art galleries, shops and studios provide visitors to Mayne the opportunity to pick up a *potlatch* (gift) for someone special. Mayne is home to a variety of fine artists, writers, artisans and filmmakers. Watch for road signs and the chance to meet an artist working in their studio.

Mayne Island Glass Foundry

The *Mayne Island Glass Foundry* is a studio where you can watch glass being blown, cast and pressed into art. It is also a small-scale, glass recycling business. The studio can be found on Aya Reach Road.

En-Vision Gallery

The *En-Vision Gallery* showcases some of British Columbia's leading craftspeople and local talent. At the time of this writing, it represented the talents of Vitreous Designs, Westcoast Gnomes, as well as of the studio potter, John Charowsky. The gallery can be found at the Fernhill Centre on Fernhill Road.

Island Elements

At the turn of the century, a Victorian style home was built at Miners Bay, on Fernhill Road. It was later converted into a gift shop, called the *Island Cottage*. At the time of this writing, it was under new management, operating as *Island Elements*.

Miners Bay Books

Miners Bay Books can be found at the historic Root Seller Inn at Miners Bay. It offers quality new and used books, gifts, cards, toys and games. The store specializes in West Coast, British Columbian, local author, children's and literary fiction.

McKenzie Fine Art Gallery

McKenzie Fine Art Gallery features the unique paintings of Jim McKenzie. McKenzie's genre is West Coast realism and his works are available in oil or print. The gallery can be found at the Fernhill Centre on Fernhill Road.

Hidden Lighthouse Gifts

In addition to providing the local Islanders with essentials, *Hidden Lighthouse Gifts and Essential*s has a variety of gifts and collectibles. You will see creations by local artists, unique and unusual gifts and things of a nautical nature. The store also sells sporting goods, and hiking and fishing equipment. It can be found on the residential property across from the Fernhill Centre, on Fernhill Road.

Tree Frog Gallery & Natural Clothing

Tree Frog Gallery & Natural Clothing specializes in items produced using organic materials. The gallery is located in the Fernhill Centre on Fernhill Road.

Events to Attend

In the year prior to this writing, a Mayne Islander boarded a ferry for Mayne, to attend a baseball game. Realizing he would be late for the game if he waited for the ferry to dock, he threw himself overboard and started swimming.[162]

Three ferries launched rescue boats in an effort to come to the man's aid. However, he refused to get into any of the boats and swam all the way to shore. Unfortunately, he never made it to the game because authorities took him to a hospital on Vancouver Island for a physical examination.[163]

Whether it is an annual event, such as the *LavenderFestival* or the *Country Fair*, or a special event, such as a music festival or play, there is always something to take in on Mayne Island.

The Mayne Island Lions Club has been active for over 30 years[164] and a few years prior to this writing, the Mayne Island Volunteer Firefighter's Association was formed[165]. Both organizations host a variety of events throughout the year.

Settlers participating in an 'egg & spoon' race in the early 1900's, BC Archives NA-40411

FoLK Night

A young musician from Vancouver, who has recorded an album under a major label, was performing at the Agriculture Hall. During his set break, he was approached by a bearded man who said, "I really like your stuff. I play music too. My name's Raffi".

The Mayne Island Folk Club was formed a few years prior to this writing. The club gets together on *Folk Night*, which is held on the first Friday of every month, at the Agricultural Hall. The stage is open to all musicians and is then followed by the feature performance of the evening. Musicians and singers like Alison Crowe, Jeremy Fisher, Rick Fines, The Gruff, etc., have all performed live at the hall.

Raffi, a beloved entertainer and songwriter, whose music has made him a friend to millions of children and their families, divides his time between a condominium on the mainland and a retreat on Mayne Island. His non-profit *Troubadour Foundation* is also based on Mayne.

Easter Egg HuNt

The annual *Easter Egg Hunt* and parade take place in March, at Dinner Bay Community Park. Each year, a Mayne Island resident dresses up as the Easter Bunny. There are also prizes for the best Easter bonnet.

MotHer'S Day PaNcaKe BreaKFaSt

At the *Mother's Day Pancake Breakfast* you can get some great *deadshot* (flapjacks). The event is held in May, at the old schoolhouse on Felix Jack Road.

CaNada Day PicNic

The *Canada Day Picnic* is celebrated on July 1 at Dinner Bay Community Park. There is food, events and a variety of festivities.

Mayne Island Farmer's Market

The Agriculture Fair Grounds are the site of the famous *Mayne Island Farmer's Market*, which runs every Saturday from July through to October. The market provides for a cornucopia of fresh produce from local farmers, as well as art from local artists and craftspeople.

Country Fair

The *Country Fair* is held early in July at St. Mary Magdalene Church. It is the church's only fundraising event. The fair

is complete with games, auctions, baked goods and entertainment.

Mayne Island Dog Show

The *Mayne Island Dog Show* is an annual event that has been taking place since the late 1990's. The event is held at the end of July, in Dinner Bay Community Park. In the year prior to this writing, there were 56 entrants in a variety of categories.

Mayne Island Fall Fair

One of Mayne's earliest female settlers started the *Mayne Island Fall Fair* in the 1920's. It grew and expanded until World War II, when it was terminated and became dormant for seven years.[166]

Today, the Mayne Island Fall Fair is the oldest fall fair in the outer Gulf Islands.[167] It takes place on the third Saturday in August, at the Agriculture Fair Grounds. There is judging in a variety of categories, from produce and baking, to photography and crafts.

The Mayne Island Fall Fair also provides for a colorful parade, great music, games, demonstrations, raffles and other special events.

FeStıvaL aveNder

Sequim, Washington is the lavender growing capital of North America, where the largest lavender festival attracts 30,000 visitors each year.

On Mayne, three women started their own lavender festival a few years prior to this writing.[168] *FestivaLavender*, which is held at Valhalla Gardens, takes place each year in August. It is much smaller than the Sequim event, but it does have good food, music, contests, and lots of lavender exhibits.

FestivaLavender features some demonstrations of a variety of products made from the lavender plant, from creams and lotions to baked goods and ice cream. Some Islanders demonstrate uses of lavender that most people will have never seen before.

MayNe ISLaNd CoW Pıe RuN

The *Mayne Island Cow Pie Run* is an annual event that has been taking place in September since the 1990's. Originally, the participants had to avoid cow pies as they ran through pastures. However, today, the run takes place entirely on pavement. At the time of this writing, the route was 8 km long and started and ended at Miners Bay.

Terry FoX RuN

In the 1980's, Terrance Fox, a 20-year-old amputee from British Columbia, inspired all Canadians with his 'Marathon of Hope', a personal run across Canada to raise funds for cancer research.[169]

A few years prior to this writing, the Mayne Island Fitness Group organized the island's first *Terry Fox Run*.[170] It has since become an annual event and in the year prior to this writing, over 100 people participated in it. Of the communities participating in British Columbia, Mayne was second in per-capita fundraising.[171]

The one, two, five or ten kilometer run, which takes place on the second Sunday after Labour Day, starts at the Georgina Point Lighthouse.[172]

QUiLt SHoW

A few years prior to this writing, 24 Canadian soldiers in Afghanistan were informed that they were going to have to spend Christmas at a remote post. Upon hearing this, the Mayne Island Quilters Guild held a 'Quilt Til You Wilt' day, donating their time and materials to make a quilt for each soldier. All 24 quilts were then shipped to where the soldiers were stationed, in time for Christmas.[173]

Earlier, that same year, busloads of quilters from surrounding areas joined the quilters guild in a quilt exhibition they called, 'Blowing In The Wind'.[174]

Every four years, the Mayne Island Quilters Guild displays their hand-made quilts in their *Quilt Show*. At the time of this writing, the guild had 50 members.[175] The show attracts quilters from all over the Gulf Islands.

SaLMoN BarbecUe

The annual *Salmon Barbecue* occurs in September, on Labour Day Sunday, at Dinner Bay Community Park. The event, which is jokingly referred to as the *Wasp Festival*, provides for barbecued salmon, beer gardens, games and entertainment.

CHristMaS CeLebratioNS

Mayne Islanders start the Christmas season off with two craft fairs, held at the Mayne Island School and Agriculture Hall. They decorate the tall Douglas-Fir tree, in Miners Bay Community Park, with lights that can be seen from boats in the Pass. The Japanese Garden, at Dinner Bay Community Park, is also decorated with lights.

For over 40 years, the Bellingham Central Lions Club, in Washington State, has been sending the *Santa Ship* to Mayne Island to bring toys and gifts to the kids.[176] After the Santa Ship is greeted, Santa and his 'helpers' are given a lift to the Agriculture Hall, where the gifts are distributed.

Mayne Islanders finish the Christmas season with a bonfire at Miners Bay Community Park, where carols are sung around the tree on Christmas Eve.

ParKS to ViSit

Mayne Island has a growing number of parks for people to enjoy. An active Parks and Recreation Commission is working on an expanded trail system, enhancing the community parks, and developing several heritage sites.

There are no provincial parks and no Crown land on Mayne. Most of the land is privately owned. Those trails that cross private land will remain available only as long as hikers respect the property rights and concerns of the owners.

Mayne Island trails range from short, seashore access, walking trails to forest hikes, so you might want to invest in a pair of *waffle stompers* (hiking shoes).

Mayne does not have its own landfill, so a private contractor must transport waste off island. As well as ensuring that nothing is left on the trails, hikers should take as much of their *iktas* (belongings) as possible off the island.

Chu-An Park

Chu-An Park is a linear park on the north side of Mayne. Chu-An, which means 'looks out over the sea', has a viewpoint that does just that. The park is accessible by way of a secret 620 m trail, of moderate difficulty, which can be found halfway down the south side of Waugh Road.

Conconi Reef Park

Conconi Reef Park provides for a pebbled beach in Gallagher Bay, on the south side of Mayne. It offers great views of neighboring Pender Island.

The beach at Conconi Reef Park is accessible via a short, easy trail at the end of Navy Channel Road. Another short, but challenging, trail exists on the north side of the road and is accessible by way of a footbridge. It provides for a spectacular view of the bay and of Pender Island.

DiNNer Bay CoMMUNity ParK

Dinner Bay Community Park was established as a recreational area in the 1980's. It is located at Dinner Bay, on the southwest side of Mayne, and is accessible by way of Williams Place.

Dinner Bay Park has a fenced playground, badminton net, horseshoe pitch, baseball diamond, picnic shelters, a beachfront swimming area and a putting green. It is the site of the *Salmon Barbecue* and of the *Canada Day Picnic* celebrations. The park grounds are maintained by the Mayne Island Community and can be rented for events and activities.

Heritage ParK

A few years prior to this writing, a man was swept off his boat called the *Espérance*, while traveling from Vancouver Island to Washington State. He was plunged into the waters approximately 6 km from Mayne Island. He was not wearing a life vest.[177]

Bravely, he heaved his *sakalooks* (pants) over his head to fill the legs with air and used them as a crude life raft. Then, he proceeded to do a slow breaststroke toward a lighthouse in the distance. He swam an exhaustive three hours until he reached the shore of *Heritage Park*.[178]

The site of the Active Pass Light Station, Heritage Park is accessible from Georgina Point Road. It is a federal, shoreline access park that is leased to the Mayne Island Parks and Recreation Commission. The park grounds are maintained by the Mayne Island Community and can be rented for art shows, book readings, weddings, etc. There are facilities for picnics if you want to stay awhile.

Heritage Park is dancing with Arbutus trees, behind which is a Dahlia Garden. The park provides for breathtaking views of the Pass and of Galiano Island. At low tide, you can walk along the beach for *lele* (a long time) looking at the Sea Stars. There is also a short, easy trail in the park, which leads to the beach.

There is also a secret access on Wilkes Road.

Marine Heritage Park

In the 1990's, a large amount of land was acquired by the Pacific Marine Heritage Legacy, a five-year program to create an expanded and integrated network of coastal and marine protected areas on the West Coast.[179]

The land it acquired included Bennett Bay and Campbell Point, as well as Georgeson Island, all of which are located on the east side of Mayne. These areas are now protected as *Marine Heritage Park*, part of the Gulf Islands National Park Reserve.[180]

Marine Heritage Park is accessible by way of an easy trail that loops around Campbell Point. The trail can be accessed from the end of Isabella Lane.

Originally named *Paddon Point*,[181] Campbell Point is highly regarded for its Arbutus trees and is a good place to see some of the most incredible examples anywhere on the West Coast.

At the end of Campbell Point, there is a view of Mount Baker, a 3,300 m strato-volcano located in Washington State. It is also a place to see Garry Oak or watch the sea lions while you picnic in the park.

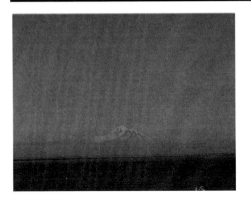

MiNerS Bay CoMMUNity Park

Miners Bay Community Park sits in the heart of Miners Bay. There are facilities for picnics if you want to stay awhile. During the Christmas season, the tall Douglas-Fir tree in the park is decorated with a spectacle of lights.

MouNt Parke RegioNaL Park

In the late 1990's, an aircraft chartered by Purolator Courier was traveling from the mainland to Victoria. As it approached Mayne, it struck some trees on the ridge of a park and sliced through

a large number of treetops. It continued over a cliff and crashed into the valley below. Both the pilot and the co-pilot were killed.[182]

Mount Parke Regional Park is a large parcel of land that was bequeathed to Mayne in the 1990's. It is dark with Western Red Cedar, Red Alder, Giant Sword-Fern and Oregon Grape. Within the park's boundaries sits a 255 m peak that is officially named Parke Mountain, but which was known locally as *Flag Hill*[183]. The peak is one of the highest points in all of the Gulf Islands.

Shortly after its establishment, the threat of large scale, commercial logging of the park caused the Mayne Island Conservancy Society to be formed. The organization ensures that the summit ridge remains part of one intact and contiguous ecosystem.[184]

From the park entrance on Montrose Road, an easy, 300 m trail leads to a junction where three other somewhat challenging trails lead into the park. All three trails total 5 km.

The trail to the left leads to a viewpoint at *Halliday Ridge*, which provides for spectacular panoramic views of Saturna, Salt Spring and Pender Islands. Beyond those smaller islands, you can see Vancouver Island, as well as the Olympic Mountains in Washington State.

> **Treasure Hunt**
> *There is a bench that has the name of The Rootseller Inn carved in it. Can you find it on Mayne Island?*

From Halliday Ridge, the hike continues deeper into the park, to the *Old Gulch Trail*. From there, you can take the *Lowland Nature Trail* straight into a nature appreciation park called *Mary Jeffrey Park*, or you can turn right at the *Arbutus Tree Trail*.

PLuMper PaSS ParK

Plumper Pass Park can be accessed by way of a 1.7 km trail that loops around the park. The trail can be accessed from Kim Road.

In the year of this writing, a second trail was constructed in the park, providing for views of the North Shore Mountains and neighboring Bowen Island. It can be accessed from Mount Parke Road.

ViLLage Bay ParK

Village Bay Park is a small park that provides for a beach on Village Bay. It can be accessed from the end of Callaghan Crescent or by way of two easy trails on Dalton Drive and Mariner's Way.

Beaches to Explore

Before the gold rush, Mayne Island and many of its surrounding bays, reefs, channels and passes were named after officers of the British Royal Navy, or their vessels.[185] Over the years, its coastline has been reshaped by the tides.

The beaches around Mayne consist primarily of sedimentary rock. Most are public property up to where the driftwood ends.

Although there are no rivers or lakes on Mayne, it has more bays than most of the other Gulf Islands. For people with car-top boats, there are various places to launch in the bays, including federal docks and public wharfs. The many coves and inlets are ideal for boat moorage, and the protected bays and shallow waters make it easy to find a cove to anchor in for the *poolakle* (night).

For experienced scuba divers, Mayne's reefs offer incredible underwater scenery.

Arbutus Bay

On the southeast side of Mayne, a challenging 300 m trail, off Beachwood Drive, leads to *Arbutus Bay*. This pristine, secluded, rocky beach is a perfect spot to watch wildlife.

BeNNett Bay

In the 1870's, a settler and his family emigrated from Scotland to Mayne. With little or no farming experience, they developed a large, successful farm on a bay on the east side.[186]

In the 1890's, the settler became the first manager of the Point Comfort Hotel. By then, his wife had become well known as the midwife of the Gulf Islands and one of their own children was the first white man born on Mayne.[187]

Bennett Bay was named after this family. It provides for glorious views of Georgeson Island. If you launch a boat from the bay, you can sail through Georgeson Passage, toward Campbell Bay, or you can head toward Horton Bay. Since it is exposed to winds, Bennett Bay offers only temporary boat anchorage.

Bennett Bay also provides for one of the finest sandy beaches in the Gulf Islands. This great *soaking* (swimming) beach can be accessed from Wilkes Road

Two smaller, rocky beaches on Bennett Bay are accessible by way of Arbutus Drive. Both of these more secluded beaches are best visited at low tide, revealing the tidal pools. They are also good spots for scuba diving at a depth of up to 12 m.

CaMpbeLL Bay

Campbell Bay is the deepest bay on Mayne. Located on the northeast side of the island, it is exposed to winds and offers only temporary boat anchorage.

Two, small, rocky beaches on Campbell Bay are accessed by way of unmarked trails on Campbell Bay Road. Because rocks that absorb the warmth of the sun surround them, these beaches provide for one of the finest swimming locations in the Gulf Islands. A small sign in the trees identifies Boulder Beach, which is clothing-optional.

CurLeW ISLaNd

Curlew Island, off the southeast side of Mayne Island, contains less than .3 sq km of land. One of the first settlers to own the island made his home there, in the 1890's. It changed owners several times. Some settlers raised goats there, which provided them with milk and cheese.

Curlew Island can be explored by way of Horton Bay. It is not serviced, except for a group of bighorn, mountain sheep. The island is infested with domesticated peacocks that are living in the wild. If you listen carefully, you can often hear them squeal.

David Cove

In the 1870's, a load of sandstone was bound for San Francisco on a schooner called the *Zephyr*. It sank in a *Squamish wind* (snowstorm) off a cove on the north side of Mayne. When it sank, it took the captain and one crewmember with it.[188]

The wreck is reported to be the oldest wreck in the Gulf Islands and is protected under the Heritage Conservation Act of British Columbia. It was not discovered until the 1970's. A decade later, a large block of sandstone, which can be seen at the Mayne Island Museum, was recovered from the wreck.[189]

The cove where the schooner sank was originally named *Hidden Bay*. It was later renamed *David Cove*, after an early Mayne settler who once lived there. Reportedly, there are two graves on the eastern peninsula beside the cove, where the settler and his daughter rest.[190]

David Cove is a beautiful inlet with a rocky beach that provides for an abundance of clams, mussels, limpets, snails and crabs. It offers some safe boat anchorage.[191]

Further out from David Cove is a favorite spot for scuba diving, where the wreck of the Zephyr exists eastward, toward Edith Point. The cove can be accessed from the end of Petrus Road.

Dinner Bay

Dinner Bay is located on the southwest side of Mayne. You can access the pebbled beach by way of steps in Dinner Bay Community Park.

The easy, 600 m *Ed Williams Memorial Trail* is accessible by way of Leighton Lane. It winds through woods and along the shore of the beach. Because it is exposed to winds and ferry wash, the mooring facilities at Dinner Bay offer only temporary boat anchorage.

Gallagher Bay

On the south side of Mayne, the shoreline at *Gallagher Bay* reveals views of nearby islands. The bay is a good spot to catch cod fish. It is also shallow with several reefs, including Conconi Reef, which make it an ideal place to scuba dive at a depth of 12 m. The bay is accessible from Navy Channel Road and offers temporary boat anchorage.

Georgeson Island

Georgeson Island is a beautiful ridge on the east side of Mayne. The southern shore of Georgeson has great sandstone formations and you can often catch sight of a Bald Eagle flying to the island across Georgeson Passage. However, Georgeson Island has been designated as a 'no access' area.

Horton Bay is located on the southeast side of Mayne. It provides for breathtaking views of Curlew Island to the east.

Horton Bay

When the first Japanese settled at *Horton Bay* in the early 1900's, it was called *Kawashuri Bay*.[192] In the 1930's, when the Japanese families formed a marketing cooperative,[193] a portable sawmill was built on the bay to provide the lumber for the crates used in the shipments of products.[194]

Today, the home of the first Japanese family to settle on Mayne still sits in a tiny cove in the bay. The family was evacuated from it at the start of World War II. It was later acquired to serve returning veterans of that same war.[195]

Because of the government wharf at the end of Horton Bay Road, Horton Bay is a great location for boat launching. However, be careful of the *skookumchuck* (strong currents), which are strongest on the east side of Curlew.

You can also put a boat in Horton Bay at a pebbled beach that is accessible by way of Steward Road. The road leads to a small point, known locally as *Spud Point.*

Maude Bay

In the 1920's, the retired Commander who had operated the Point Comfort Hotel and the Mayne Store attempted to sail his sailboat, the *Half Moon*, from Mayne to England, alone. He was 77 years of age.[196]

The Commander, who had once served on Queen Victoria's own, personal yacht,[197] had spent over 100 days at sea and had traveled over 6,000 km when he was caught in a storm off the coast of San Francisco. The storm caused the boom to strike him on the head and left him unconscious. He was rescued by a freighter and returned to his home on Mayne, only to succeed in his journey the following year.[198]

The Commander's eccentric wife used to walk to the church in the early morning hours, where she would play the organ in complete darkness.[199]

Reportedly, *Maude Bay* was named after this family - the first British middle-class family to settle on Mayne.[200]

You can see a wide variety of sea life on Maude Bay. Mussels, oysters, limpets and crabs abound. The bay is also known as *Cherry Tree Bay*.[201] From Cherry Tree Bay Road, you can make your way down to the rocky beach using a charming, but broken-down, old dock.

Miners Bay

By the 1890's, **the Postman** had become a member of the Islands Agricultural and Fruit Growers Association.[202] Although his fruit sold well, eventually, Okanagan fruit proved superior and the Mayne market died.[203]

Today, there are still ancient fruit trees growing along the trail that leads to the pebbled beach at *Miners Bay*. The beach exists in front of **the Postman's** first home. The short trail to the beach also provides for great berry picking. You can access it at the end of Naylor Road.

If you walk beneath the wharf at Miners Bay, you can watch the water as it falls down the rocks at the base of the Springwater Lodge. Although it has limited space and strong tides, you can find docking facilities at the wharf, from which you can walk into the village.

Oyster Bay

On the northern tip of Mayne is *Oyster Bay*. On its rocky beach are interesting driftwood and rock formations. Mussels, limpets, oysters and crabs are plentiful, and there is a good supply of snails in the shallow pool.

Further out from Oyster Bay, Georgina Shoals is one of the best places to scuba dive in the Gulf Islands, at a depth of 10 m. You can access the bay from Bayview Drive.

Piggott Bay

In the 1890's, an early settler from Pender Island left his brother and moved to Mayne. Whenever he wanted to visit his brother, he would walk to what was then called *Brigg's Landing*, at *Piggott Bay*. There, he would light a fire, or blow a horn made out of a bull kelp, in order to get his brother's attention. His brother would then row over from Pender to pick him up.[204]

Located on the south side of Mayne, Piggott Bay provides for a shallow, sandy beach lined with large pieces of driftwood. Clams are also plentiful. Because of its warm waters, it is a great place for a swim.

You can access Piggott Bay from the end of Piggott Road. Because it is exposed to the winds, it offers only temporary boat anchorage.

ReeF Bay

Reef Bay is located between Oyster Bay and David Cove, on the north side of Mayne. It is dotted with pieces of driftwood. Mussels, snails, limpets and crabs are plentiful. The rocky beach can be accessed from Bayview Drive.

Village Bay

Because the First Nations *rancherie* (village) existed on the southwest side of Mayne Island in the 1860's, the area eventually became known as *Village Bay*. All of the people who lived there were called *skeh-SUCK* (the Pass) people.[205]

In the 1880's, as Miners Bay was being settled, a prominent Mayne settler purchased a large farm sitting in a valley at Village Bay. His family built a home at the edge of their farm, overlooking the bay.[206]

A decade later, the family converted their home into a very popular resort they called *Kitty's Boarding House*.[207]

Barn at Village Bay in the 1950's, BC Arcihves NA-40412

When **the Postman** passed away in the early 1900's, the family took over his post office, which was operating from the store beside his home at Miners Bay.[208]

A few years later, the family's boarding house was destroyed by fire.[209] Today, the barn is the only building that remains of their large farm and resort.

Barn at Village Bay as it appears today

In the 1950's, an end-loading ferry terminal was built at Village Bay, where the resort once stood.[210] For the most part, it replaced the wharf at Miners Bay.[211]

In the 1960's, a ferry linking the mainland to Salt Spring Island was introduced, making the Gulf Islands more accessible. This caused Mayne Island's population to double over the next decade.[212]

The Village Bay terminal, early 1960's, BC Ferries Archives

In the 1980's, a second dock was added to the terminal, allowing vehicles to transfer from one ferry to another. This made Village Bay an important transfer point for the Gulf Islands routes.[213]

Today, British Columbia Ferry Services uses the land at Village Bay to operate scheduled ferry services from both the mainland and Vancouver Island. At the time of this writing, it reported carrying 3.5 million passengers throughout the southern Gulf Islands each year.

Treasure Hunt
A prominent Mayne settler developed a farm called Hardscrabble. Can you find it on Mayne Island?

The Village Bay terminal as it appears today

You can access the pebbled beach at Village Bay from the end of Callaghan Crescent. If you launch a boat from the bay, a cruise along the shoreline to Dinner Point is quite scenic. Keep in mind that ferry traffic is heavy in the bay.

Because it is exposed to winds and ferry wash, the mooring facilities offer only temporary anchorage for boaters.

PLaceS to FISH

Early Mayne Island settlers fished the Pass from their boats. They could catch several salmon in only an hour or two. They also caught plenty of herring and cod. Their catch never went to waste. It was always passed around to *tillicum* (friends).[214]

Early settlers with salmon caught from Active Pass, Salt Spring Archives G-01

Today, Mayne Island is famous for some of the greatest Spring and Coho salmon fishing in the world. Salmon fishing in the Strait is a year-round sport, with the best fishing occurring in winter.

The Pass is also a prized salmon-fishing ground, providing the best summer fishing in the Gulf Islands. It is a crossroads for salmon returning to spawn in the Fraser River, which has the world's largest, natural, salmon runs.

One of the best ways to determine the whereabouts of salmon is to watch the action of the birds on the surface. Birds feeding on the surface indicate that there are baitfish below.

Keep in mind that the excellent fishing in the Pass occurs during months when the ferry traffic is at its highest, and accidents between ferries and sport fishermen have occurred there.

You can also fish for salmon between St. John Point and Conconi Reef, on the southeast side of Mayne. If the salmon fishing is slow, you can try fishing for other bottom fish, such as Ling Cod, Red Snapper, Black Bass and Sole.

If you want to try your hand at fishing, fishing rods can be obtained at Hidden Lighthouse Gifts and Essentials on Fernhill Road. Fishing licenses, tackle and bait can be obtained at the gas station at Miners Bay.

If you decide to let someone else do the fishing, you can purchase freshly caught shellfish and salmon fillets from the *MV Armada*, which periodically docks at Miners Bay.

Active Pass Fishing Charters

Active Pass Fishing Charters provides guided salmon fishing charters aboard a 7 m boat. All fishing rods and reels are supplied. The boat can accommodate up to three guests. Phone (250) 539-5034

Wildlife to Observe

The wildlife found on Mayne Island is very diverse. Although the Pass is a great place to watch wildlife and is most spectacular in the spring, many species are commonly seen throughout the year. However, because some are more elusive and it requires a bit of luck to spot them, only the most commonly seen species have been listed in this book.

Marine Mammals

Marine mammals have adapted characteristics to survive and prosper in environments that are hostile to most land mammals. Some migrate from Mayne to tropical habitats that are suitable for birthing. Northern migrations begin early in the spring and southern migrations begin in the fall.

The Orca Pass initiative is a citizen-led project whereby both Canada and the United States have agreed to cooperate on the preservation and protection of the Orca Pass International Stewardship Area. This area is a delicate marine mammal and sea-life environment around Mayne and the other Gulf Islands.

Harbour Porpoises, or Common Porpoises, are small whales that only grow to 1.8 m in length. They are brown to black in color, with a white underside. They can frequently be seen swimming through the Pass.

Harbour Seals, also known as Common Seals or Leopard Seals, can grow to 1.8 m in length. They are gray with a unique pattern of fine, dark spots. They have a whiskery nose and bulging eyes. Their hind flippers extend backwards.

Harbour Seals favor quiet, rocky places that they can land on during low tide. They are the marine mammals you are most likely to see around Mayne, but they will dive into the water if they are approached too closely. You can often see seals swimming through the Pass.

Orcas, also known as Killer Whales, Black Fish or Grampus, are actually dolphins. They are black with a white chest and sides. They sport a white patch above and behind the eye. They can grow to 9.5 m in length and weigh as much as 10,000 kilograms.

The coast of British Columbia is well known as the place on *Elehe* (Earth) to watch migrating and resident whales feeding and breaching. They are usually seen in pods of 5-25 animals. The best time to see the Orca is in the Pass during the summer.

Pacific White-Sided Dolphin are greenish-black with grey stripes along their sides. They have a white belly. They can grow to a length of 2.5 m. Large groups of dolphin readily approach boats in the Pass, particularly in the spring and fall. Fishermen often refer to them as 'lags'.

Sea Lions can grow to 3 m in length and weigh 1,000 kg. They are brown to black in color. Some species were put on the U.S. endangered species list in the 1990's and have since been the object of intense study. Some species are intelligent and adaptable, and are often trained as entertainers at ocean parks and zoos.

Around Mayne, sea lions delight in flinging kelp around, and body surfing in waves around Georgeson Island and the Belle Chain Islets to the east. They can also be seen at the west end of the Pass, either in the water or hauled up on the rocks on Helen Point.

Otters are reddish-brown to black in color. They are intelligent and very playful, frequently floating and swimming on their backs. Although they were once near extinction, otters have begun to spread again, along the coast. The otters around Mayne are actually river otters, not sea otters. Some of the best places to spot them are at the Miners Bay wharf and at Arbutus Bay.

Sea Life

The ocean environment around Mayne supports a delicate, yet complex web of life. When the tide recedes, the depressions that retain water between the rocks are called *tidal pools*. Tidal pools are natural aquariums for an abundance of vertebrates and invertebrates. *Siwash loggers* (beachcombers) can see this life when the tide goes out.

For those who want to gather filter-feeding shellfish from around Mayne, a permit is required to dig and quantities are limited. Permits can be obtained at the gas station at Miners Bay.

Clams, or Macoma, can live for 20 years or more. Although the Smooth Washington Clam supports the clam industry, there are several varieties around Mayne, most of which are white in color.

If you find a clam shell on the beach surface, the clam is no longer living in it. However, finding live *luk'-ut-chee* (clams) is not difficult if you look in mixed mud, rock and sand. The smallest clams, called *Little-Necks*, can be found just beneath the surface. The larger *Butter Clams*, which can live for 20 years, can be found about 20 cm from the surface. The largest and longest-living clams, called *Horse Clams*, can be found about 30 cm from the surface.[215]

Clams feed, breathe and expel waste through tubes that extend from the clam to the surface of the beach, so you can tell if there are clams embedded in a beach if you see water squirting out of the sand. One of the best places to dig for clams around Mayne is Piggott Bay at low tide. A small shovel or hand rake works well to uncover them.

Crabs prefer a sand or mud bottom. They are reddish-brown to purple in color. Some species of crab can grow to a width of 23 cm and can live for 6 years.

You need a trap to actually land crabs that are large enough to eat and catching crabs is a secret kept by *island crabbers* (Mayne Islanders who catch crab). However, you can see small specimens in shallow waters on Maude Bay, Oyster Bay and Reef Bay. In fact, most of the movement you see in tidal pools are crabs scurrying about.

Cockles look somewhat like clams. They are cream-colored with a grey or brown mottled pattern. They have deeply set ridges, which make them easy to identify. Cockles can often be found on or near the surface of muddy or sandy beaches. You can find them on Maude Bay, Oyster Bay and Reef Bay.

Some species can live for up to 16 years.

Jellyfish are not actually fish. They are a member of the invertebrate family. They feed on small fish and zooplankton that become caught in their tentacles where stinging cells latch onto them.

Jellyfish are usually found floating near the surface of the water or stranded on the beach. You can find jellyfish at Bennett Bay and at Miners Bay. Some species of jellyfish at Miners Bay are among the largest in the world and can grow to 50 cm in diameter.

Limpets have an elliptical shell that rises to a peak. Unlike mussels, clams and oysters, limpets have only one shell half, which is usually greenish brown with cream lines radiating down from the peak. The underside has a brown spot in the center.

Limpets attach themselves to the sides of the rocks along the shoreline. There are good supplies of limpets at Oyster Bay and on Georgina Point.

Mussels found on Mayne are generally dark blue with hints of brown. They can grow to 20 cm in length. They attach themselves to rocks and to wood, especially to pilings.

One of the best places to find colonies of *to'-luks* (mussels) around Mayne is at Oyster Bay. To gather them, just locate a colony and pry them loose. As you gather them, make sure the shells are closed tightly or that they snap shut when you grab them.

Oysters are greyish-white in color. Their shells are wavy and mold to the object they attach themselves to. They can grow to 30 cm in length. The Japanese introduced some of the oysters on Mayne, in the 1920's.

The *klógh-klogh* (oyster) can be found attached to rocks on the beach surface. To gather them, you must pry them loose with a sharp tool. Some of the best places to find oyster beds are at Maude Bay, Oyster Bay and Reef Bay. If you harvest a supply of oysters, consider leaving the shells on the beach for new generations of oysters.

Sea Stars, or Starfish, around Mayne are usually purple in color, but can also be a bright coral color. They can grow to over 36 cm in diameter. One of the best places to find sea stars is on Georgina Point at low tide.

Sea Stars are carnivores that feed on mussels and barnacles. They flip their stomach out through their mouth and digest their prey from the inside out.

Snails have long, cylindrical-shaped shells that are gray to brown in color and often have a stripe winding around them. They only grow to 3 cm, but they can live for 10 years. You can find them in shallow water on Oyster Bay and Reef Bay. The Japanese accidentally introduced some species of snails to the Gulf Islands, in the 1920's.

Land Mammals

In the early 1900's, large mammals, such as cougars, bears and wolves, were flushed out of Mayne and the other Gulf Islands by hound dogs. They were then shot.[216] Since hunting is no longer permitted on Mayne, except by bow and arrow, land mammals are relatively tame.

Columbia Blacktail Deer, or Mowich, are a small sub-species of mule deer. They are the largest land mammals you are likely to see on Mayne. Unfortunately, as cute as they are, deer eliminate the forest understory in their search for food and are common enough to support Mayne's fence builders. You can find them just about everywhere.

Douglas Squirrels, or Chickaree, are brown rodents with a bushy tail and a distinctive call. They make their home in tree cavities or in nests constructed of twigs, needles and bark. You can see them leaping from branch to branch in Mayne's dense forests.

Raccoons have soft, dense, grey fur and a black mask across their face. They have long tails that are characterized by a pattern of rings. You can see raccoons along some of the beaches around Mayne. Their presence is revealed by human-like handprints, which can be seen in the mud.

Townsend's Chipmunks are brown rodents with black stripes. Because they seldom climb trees, they move along the ground. Chipmunks hibernate during the winter months. In the summer, you can see them in Mayne's dense forests.

Western Spotted Skunks have soft, black fur. They are distinctively marked with white spots on their forehead, and white stripes on their back and sides. You can find skunks on the farmlands around Mayne.

Birds

Mayne Island is well known for its bird watching opportunities. Its rocky shores are stopover sites for migratory birds and nesting sites for many sea birds.

Over 130 species of marine birds from 22 countries breed, migrate and/or spend the winter in the Strait. The climate invites them to reside or visit, so, in the winter, Mayne becomes a *kalakala* (bird) watchers' paradise.

Bald Eagles have a white head and tail, and a contrasting brown body. They can grow to 90 cm tall with a wingspan of 2 m. Although they are indigenous to North America, they were on the brink of extinction late in the 20th century. Fortunately, they have largely recovered and, today, 25 percent of the world's eagle nesting population is found in British Columbia.

Eagles are birds of prey. Their main food supply is the Glaucous-Winged Gull. In the summer, they search for surface-feeding fish, snatching food with aerial acrobatics. They are also good at forcing other birds to drop their prey and will often steal prey from an Osprey.

'Baldies' are commonly seen around Mayne, especially in the spring when they are rearing their young. Those that are old enough to nest often return to the area in which they were raised. Their nests, which are protected by law, can span 3 m across and weigh 900 kg.

Because they prefer nest sites with a view, you can see them on Campbell Point as they fly across Georgeson

Passage. You can also spot them in Chu-An Park and gathering in the Pass.

Belted Kingfishers have deep blue or bluish-gray plumage with white markings. They have a broad white collar around their neck and a blue band around their chest. The blue feathers on their heads make their heads appear larger than they are.

The Belted Kingfisher is the only species of kingfisher found in the Pacific Northwest. As loners, they only tolerate one another at mating time. Whenever there is good fishing around Mayne, you can expect to find them perched on trees or posts, close to the water. They are a noisy bird with a loud, rattling call.

Gulls are graceful in flight, voracious when feeding and capable of many sounds. One small, delicate species is most often seen on Mayne in winter. However, other species can be found, year-round. The best place to find gulls is in the Pass.

Brown Creepers have a mottled brown coloration and long, stiff tail-feathers. Their cheerful song has been described as 'trees, trees, trees, see the trees'.

Brown Creepers are common, year-round residents of the forests on Mayne. A creeper will typically forage upwards on tree bark. As it nears the treetop, it drops to the base of a nearby tree to begin its ascent all over again. If it is frightened, it will flatten itself against the tree trunk, becoming almost impossible to see.

Canada Geese have a black head and neck. They have a broad, white chin strap with a contrasting brown body. In flight, they slice through the skies in 'V-formations' or in long lines.

Canada Geese mate for life and are faithful to their breeding grounds, returning to their birth sites each spring. They are abundant waterfowl that can be found year-round. One of the best places to find them on Mayne is at Bennett Bay.

Cormorants are dark, long-necked diving birds with long bills. They often stand upright and hold their wings out to dry. They can be seen flying in single file, floating low in the water, or hanging out on rocks or pilings. One species migrates north in the fall, by the thousands. You can find cormorants on Helen Point and Georgina Point.

Great Blue Herons, also known as a Shagpoke or Shikspoke, are long-legged, greyish-blue, wading birds. They can grow to 1.2 m tall with a 2 m wingspan. They have a plume of black feathers behind their eye.

Great Blue Herons can be seen standing like sentinels, gazing into the water at low tide, in search of food. They feed in shallow water and spear fish or frogs with their long, sharp bills. They will also raid goldfish ponds in Islanders' backyards. You can hear them croak as they fly laboriously to their enormous nests of sticks.

The herons found on Mayne and the other Gulf Islands are a distinctive subspecies. They are year-round residents. Some of the best places to find the heron are on Georgina Point and at Bennett Bay.

Grouse generally have a brown camouflage pattern. Some species are so well camouflaged that they allow humans, and even predators, to approach very closely. Grouse are year-round, ground-dwelling residents of Mayne's forests. Coastal peoples used to hunt grouse so they could boil them in a soup.[217]

Ospreys are mostly white underneath, with contrasting dark coloration above. They display a dark line through their eye. Most Ospreys depart Mayne in the fall and return in the spring. You can find them along the shoreline.

Ospreys are aggressors and birds of prey. An Osprey will attack an eagle if it comes too close to its nest. When an Osprey sees a fish in the water, it will suddenly tuck in its wings and plummet down, throwing its feet forward at the last minute. It will then grasp the fish with its talons and carry it with its head forward, to cut down on wind resistance. For this reason, some people refer to them as 'fish hawks'.

Pacific Loons are dark brown with a white belly. They are diving birds, preferring areas of strong currents, where they dive for fish. Sometimes, in the spring, hundreds of them can be seen diving in the Pass. In summer, they display a velvety grey head, a dark throat and a checkered back.

In winter, Pacific Loons display a border between the front and the back of their neck. Some of North America's largest wintering population exists on Mayne and the other Gulf Islands. They arrive in the fall from their northern breeding grounds.

Red-Breasted Nuthatches are small, short-tailed birds with sharp beaks. They have a black cap with a white eye stripe and a bit of rusty coloring on their chest. When they are building a nest, their hammering can sound like that of a woodpecker.

Unlike the Brown Creeper, nuthatches spiral down tree trunks, headfirst, pulling insects out of the bark. They will stay close to home year-round if there is enough food or a bird feeder in the area. They can be found in mature, cone-bearing forests around Mayne, where their call is a familiar sound.

Red-Tailed Hawks have broad wings and a broad, rust-colored tail. They are designed for soaring on thermals of warm, rising air. They are birds of prey and will eat almost any small animal. The blood-curdling scream of a Red-Tailed Hawk is what is often heard in the movies. They can be found virtually everywhere on Mayne, year-round.

Rufous Hummingbirds can fly right, left, up, down, backwards and even upside down. When hovering, they hold their bodies upright and flap their wings horizontally in a 'figure eight'. They flap their wings 12,000 times per minute, which is why they are seen as a blur.

In early spring, Rufous Hummingbirds leave their wintering grounds in Mexico and make their way north, flower by flower, sucking the nectar from the bloom of the Red-Flowering Currant and Salmonberry shrubs. A long, stiletto bill assists them in this lifestyle. They can be found in Mayne's forests and gardens.

Steller's Jays are the avian emblem of British Columbia. They are deep bluish-black in color and are frequently mistaken for the eastern Blue Jay. They have a dark crest that raises and lowers to indicate their state of agitation.

Announcing their arrival with a raucous call, Steller's Jays will descend upon a bird feeder, scattering smaller birds from it. As year-round residents that live on Mayne's forest slopes, they also like to grab acorns from trees, such as Garry Oak.

Turkey Vultures have two-toned wings and a naked, red head. They are birds of prey that are usually seen in flight with wings in a 'V-formation'. Their tilting flight is an energy-saving strategy. Without turning it's head, a Turkey Vulture can see views of the land below. It will spiral upwards within a thermal of warm, rising air, then descend in a long glide to catch the next thermal.

In the fall, Turkey Vultures use Mayne and the other Gulf Islands as stepping stones as they head south to California and Mexico. One of the best places to find them is perched in the trees along Campbell Point.

Creatures to Cook

In the gold-mining camps of the late 1800's, an expensive egg omelet, called the *Hangtown Fry*, was prepared for hungry gold miners. It contained fried breaded oysters and bacon.[218]

Seafood is incredibly easy to prepare. With a little basic knowledge, you can become an expert in no time at all. The most important thing to remember when cooking seafood is not to overcook it. It is also very important to pay strict attention to the health advisories, as paralytic shellfish poisoning is potentially deadly.

FISH

The freshness and flavor of a fish, such as salmon, cod and sole, can be preserved all day by killing it immediately and keeping it cool. To clean the fish, simply slice it lengthwise and remove the gills, as well as the contents of the carcass. Then, wash the fish before wrapping it in paper.

After the fish has been cleaned, cut through the backbone so you can *butterfly it* (spread the two sides down) on a grill or frying pan. Simmer the fish over low heat until the bones can be pulled away from the meat.

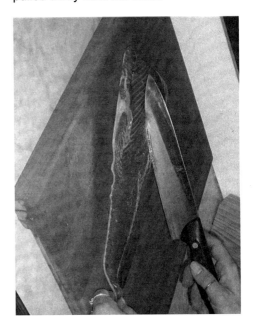

Crab

A crab should be kept alive until it is time to cook it. Before you cook a crab, first remove its shell. To remove the shell, point the crab away from your body, and grasp its legs and pinchers with your hands facing up. Hit it against a hard surface so the top of its shell lifts off. Then, simply break the crab in half and discard the contents of the carcass. To cook the carcass, just boil it and serve it with melted butter for dipping.

Clams and Mussels

To cook clams or mussels, just drop them into a pot of boiling water and leave them until their shells open. Discard the green substance from the shells of the clams. Once they have been removed from their shells, you can fry them in butter, or cook them in a pot with bacon, potatoes and milk.

Oysters

It is best to *shuck* (open) oysters right on the beach and leave the shells there for new generations of oysters. Shucked oysters can then be fried with Worcestershire sauce or added to a chowder. They can even be eaten raw.

If you prefer to cook your oysters, just throw them on hot coals with the cupped half of the shell up and leave them until their shells open.

Flora to Appreciate

Mayne Island's unique environment is host to a wide diversity of plant life. The flora on Mayne and the other Gulf Islands is probably the most varied in all of British Columbia. The National Park system is currently being expanded to include all the public lands and parks contained in the area, as protected public assets.

Mayne Island sits in one of the smallest climate zones in the west. In this zone, the rain shadow holds rainfall to less than 75 cm annually, whereas Pacific storms drench the rest of the Strait. The climate zone is noted for its beautiful, spring, wild flowers, over 250 of which grow and flourish on Mayne - too many to list in this little book.

Trees

Mayne Island is part of the coastal, Douglas-Fir, plant community, which is marked by the predominance of three trees; Douglas-Fir, Arbutus and Garry Oak. This community has a very limited range, which includes only southeastern Vancouver Island, Mayne and the other

Gulf Islands, as well as Washington State.

Amabilis means *lovely*. The Amabilis Fir, or Silver Fir, is a tall, straight tree that can grow to 55 m in height. It has flat needles that are dark and shiny. The underside of the needles show white lines that control water loss.

Arbutus, or Madrona, are Canada's only native, broad-leaved evergreen and exist on only a very small portion of the extreme West Coast. They are indigenous to Mayne and the other Gulf Islands.

The unusual Arbutus tree produces bright red berries. It sheds its thin,

smooth, cinnamon-colored bark. Although they are deciduous, Arbutus do not drop their leaves in the winter.

First Nations believe that the survivors of the *Great Flood* used the Arbutus tree to anchor their canoe to the top of Mount Newton on Vancouver Island. You can find fine examples of Arbutus on Campbell Point, as well as in Heritage Park and St. Mary Magdalene's church yard.

Bitter Cherry are small trees that produce pinkish flowers. The flowers develop into bright red, bitter cherries.

First Nations peeled off the stringy bark of the Bitter Cherry for wrapping harpoon and arrow joints.

Black Cottonwood is a hardy tree with a straight trunk. It can grow to 50 m tall. It has large, sticky, fragrant buds. The Black Cottonwood is named for the white hairs on its seeds, which float through the air like wisps of cotton.

First Nations made canoes from cottonwood. Some tribes produced soap from the inner bark. The Hudson's Bay Company reportedly continued using this method in their own brand of soaps.

Black Hawthorn is a small tree that produces white flowers. The flowers develop into small, edible, blackish-purple fruits that are shaped like apples. The thorns of the Black Hawthorn were used by First Nations as pieces for playing games.

Broadleaf Maple, or Bigleaf Maple, is the largest maple tree in Canada, reaching heights of 36 m. Its leaves measure up to 30 cm across. It is restricted to the southwest corner of British Columbia.

First Nations called the Broadleaf Maple the *Paddle Tree* because they made paddles out of the wood.

Cascara is a small tree that produces small, greenish-yellow flowers that develop into bluish-black berries. First

Nations boiled the bark of the cascara into a tea that was drank as a strong laxative.

Pacific Dogwood is an irregular tree that produces white flowers with purple tips. The flowers develop into clusters of bright red berries. The blossom of the dogwood is the floral emblem of British Columbia.

Pacific Dogwood is one of the few plants protected by the law in British Columbia. However, in spite of the protection it receives, it has often been illegally cut down. Once abundant on Mayne, most of the Pacific Dogwood has now all but vanished from the island.

Douglas-Fir, also known as the Oregon Pine or Nootka Pine, is the dominant species of tree on Mayne. It can be found just about everywhere. It can grow to 85 m high and 2 m wide. Its bark is very thick and deeply grooved.

First Nations had many uses for Douglas-Fir. They used it to make fish

hooks and handles. They used the wood and boughs as fuel for cooking. Its boughs were frequently used for covering the floors of lodges.

The Grand Fir is also found on Mayne. It is easily distinguished from other fir trees by its flat needle sprays that grow in two rows.

Garry Oaks, or Oregon White Oaks, are picturesque, gnarled, hardwood trees. They can grow to 20 m in height and can live for up to 500 years. Oaks have thick, grooved, greyish-black bark. They produce small acorns with a scaly cup on one end.

In Canada, Garry Oak are found almost exclusively on southeastern Vancouver Island, and on Mayne and the other Gulf Islands. Unfortunately, their numbers are in decline throughout the range.

Typically, the Garry Oak forms open parkland and meadows. However, from the time Mayne Island was first settled until the 1950's, much of the land that contained the oak was either logged or converted to farms. Although there are some mature oaks on Mayne, there are no significant Garry Oak meadows.

Many Garry Oak woodlands are being choked out by cone-bearing trees, which grow faster, creating shade where the oak cannot regenerate. As a result, less than five percent of the original Garry Oak habitat remains.

You can find small examples of Garry Oak at the end of Campbell Point. At the time of this writing, Mayne Islanders were proposing to create a park, at the corner of Felix Jack Road and Village Bay Road, which would contain a Garry Oak meadow.

Lodgepole Pine trees are commonly cut down for Christmas trees. They can grow to 40 m in height. Their cones often remain closed for years and open from the heat of a fire. This allows them to develop rapidly after a forest fire.

The Western White Pine is also found on Mayne. It is a symmetrical tree that can grow to 40 m in height, or taller. It is a five-needle pine. First Nations called it the *Dancing Tree*. They boiled its bark into a tea, which they drank to treat tuberculosis and rheumatism.

In the early 1900's, a shipment of Eastern White Pine was imported to the mainland from France. It carried a fungus called White Pine Blister Rust, which kills young Western White Pine trees. The fungus spread to Mayne and the other Gulf Islands so quickly that, by the 1920's, it was established throughout most of the tree range.[219]

Pacific Crabapple trees produce pinkish, fragrant, apple blossoms. The blossoms develop into small, reddish apples that are somewhat tart. During preservation, the apples become sweeter.

> **Treasure Hunt**
> *There is an Arbutus tree growing in the middle of the road. Can you find it on Mayne Island?*

Pacific Willow are tall, slender trees with pale yellow leaves associated with a flower. Although they only grow to 12 m tall, they are one of the largest native willows on the West Coast.

Red Alder is an aggressive, fast-growing hardwood tree that does not live much past 50 years. The wood of the alder provides one of the best fuels for smoking fish. One of the best places to find Red Alder is at Mount Parke Regional Park.

Sitka Spruce, or Airplane Spruce, are large trees that commonly grow to 70 m tall and 2 m across. First Nations used them extensively. They fashioned watertight hats and baskets from the roots, which also provided materials for ropes and fishing line.

Western Hemlock is a large tree that can grow to 50 m tall. It has sweeping branches and feathery foliage. Unfortunately, its shallow rooting system makes it susceptible to being blown over by wind or damaged by fire.

Because the wood of the Western Hemlock is very easy to work with, some First Nations carved it into dishes. Other tribes scraped off the inner bark and baked it into cakes.

Mountain Hemlock also grows on Mayne. It has drooping branches that have an upward sweep at the tip. In dense forests, its needles form flat sprays.

Western Red Cedar, or Canoe Cedar, is British Columbia's official tree. It is very aromatic and has graceful, swooping branches. The cedar can grow to 60 m tall and its trunk spreads widely at its base.

The cedar was considered the *Tree Of Life* by the First Nations who used its wood for dugout canoes, boxes, tools and paddles. From the inner bark, they made rope, clothing, and baskets. Most of their dwellings were constructed of large boards split from cedar logs.

Western Red Cedars live a long life, sometimes to over 1,000 years. As a result, they can be found just about everywhere on Mayne. Some of the best places to see large examples is in Mount Parke Regional Park and at Valhalla Gardens.

The Yellow-Cedar is also found on Mayne. It is the oldest tree in the area. Some are 1,500 years old. However, unlike the Western Red Cedar, the crushed leaves of the Yellow-Cedar smell like give off a mildew.

Western Yew, or Pacific Yew, is a small evergreen tree that has reddish, papery bark. Its trunk is often twisted and fluted. Although the yew is a cone-bearing tree, it produces a single seed.

A bright red, fleshy cup, which looks like a large berry, surrounds the seed. Beware of the seed, as it is poisonous.

The tough wood of the Western Yew was highly prized by First Nations. Because it displays a polished surface, it was used for carving.

Shrubs and Ferns

A characteristic feature of the shrubs on Mayne is the variety and abundance that exist in the Heather family. These shrubs dominate the understory of Mayne's mature forests, as well as in non-forested habitats. Many of the shrubs give way to edible *olali* (berries). First Nations ate these berries raw or boiled into cakes.

Black Raspberry, or Blackcap, is an erect shrub that has stems with curved prickles. It produces pinkish flowers that develop into hairy, purplish-black berries that are very tasty.

Black Twinberry, or Bearberry Honeysuckle, is an erect to straggly shrub. It produces yellow, tubular flowers, which develop into pairs of shiny, black, inedible berries.

Bog Cranberry is a dwarf shrub that only grows to 40 cm tall. It produces deep pink flowers that have petals that bend backwards. Its berries are pale pink to dark red in color.

Bracken Fern has a stout stem with a feathery frond. Its fronds were used by First Nations as a protective layer in food storage containers, on berry-drying racks and in pit ovens.

Copperbush is a leafy shrub with loose, shredding, copper-colored bark. Its flowers are also copper-colored. Its fruit develop as round capsules. It is one of only a few of the plants in its classification found exclusively in Western North America.

Devil's Club is an erect to sprawling shrub. It has thick, crooked stems that are often entangled and armed with numerous, large, yellowish spines. The wood of the shrub has a sweet smell. Its leaves are shaped like that of a maple leaf and it produces white flowers.

Related to the Ginseng plant, Devil's Club is one of the most important of all medicinal plants. Sticks made from Devil's Club were used by First Nations as protective charms. When burned, the charcoal from this shrub was used to make face paint for dancers and for tattoo ink.

Dull Oregon Grape is a common, low-growing evergreen shrub with leaves that resemble that of holly. Bright yellow flowers appear in the spring, followed by dark purple, edible berries in the summer. The berries make great jelly. Tall Oregon Grape is another shrub that can be found on Mayne, but in drier areas.

Evergreen Huckleberry has branches that bear leathery leaves lined with sharp teeth. Its clusters of pink flowers produce black berries with a flavor similar to that of a blueberry. Black Mountain Huckleberry is also found on Mayne. It thrives in old burned sites that have only sparse tree regeneration. You can find huckleberry on Campbell Point.

False Azalea, or False Huckleberry, is an erect to straggly, spreading shrub, which resembles both the Azalea plant, as well as huckleberry plants. It produces pink to yellow flowers, which develop into inedible fruit. The leaves turn a bright crimson color in the fall.

False Box is a low, dense, evergreen shrub that resembles the Kinnikinnick plant. It produces tiny, maroon colored flowers that have a pleasant fragrance. It has reddish-brown branches that are often used in floral arrangements.

Goats' Beard, or Spaghetti Flower, is a robust rose bush. It produces white flower clusters that resemble goats' beards. First Nations used the roots for medicinal purposes.

Gummy Gooseberry is an erect to spreading shrub with sticky leaves. It produces reddish colored flowers in drooping clusters. Its flowers, which produce nectar that is eaten by hummingbirds, develop into dark purple, hairy berries. The Wild Gooseberry, which produces green or purple flowers, can also be found on Mayne.

Gorse is a non-native shrub with vicious spines that can form impenetrable thickets. Unlike most plants that grow poorly in soils low in nitrogen, it can remove nitrogen from the air. This enables it to thrive in soils that are low in nitrogen. Gorse is a fire hazard.

Hairy Manzanita is an erect or spreading evergreen with very hairy leaves. Its branches have reddish-brown bark that peels. It produces pinkish flowers in hairy clusters. Manzanita means *little apples*, which describes its edible, coffee colored berries.

Hardhack, or Steeplebush, is an erect, leggy shrub with many woolly branches. It produces rose colored flowers in a long, narrow cluster. Its fruit develop as clusters of numerous, small, pod-like follicles.

Himalayan Blackberry is an immigrant species from India. It has sharp, curved spines that make this precursor of barbed wire a plant to be treated with respect. Mayne Islanders pull the deadly branches towards them using a straightened coat hanger.

Himalayan Blackberry produces fine white or pink flowers. The fruit, which is a favorite among berry pickers, is easily mistaken for a raspberry. However, unlike the blackberry, the fruit of the raspberry is hollow when picked.

The Himalayan Blackberry grows in abundance on Mayne. It is particularly accessible on Naylor Road and down the trail to the beach at Miners Bay.

Indian-Plum, or Osoberry, is a tall shrub with purplish-brown bark. It is one of the first plants to flower in the spring, at which time it produces greenish-white flowers in long clusters. Its flowers, which have an unusual scent, are produced before its leaves appear. Its fruit, which is often referred to as *choke-cherries*, resembles small plums.

Kinnikinnick, or Common Bearberry, is a creeping, evergreen, ground cover that forms dense mats. It has small, pinkish flowers. The flowers produce bright red, berries that resemble miniature apples.

Mock Orange is an erect shrub with peeling bark. It produces broad, white, fragrant flowers that develop into oval, woody fruit. First Nations used the wood for making bows and arrows.

Ocean Spray, also called Creambush or Ironwood, is an erect shrub with peeling bark. It produces creamy flowers in dense clusters that resemble lilacs. The flowers remain on the plant over the winter. The strong wood of the shrub was used by First Nations to make knitting needles and other tools.

Orange Honeysuckle, also called Ghost's Swing or Owl's Swing, is a climbing vine that can reach 6 m in height. It produces long, orange, trumpet-shaped flowers with a sweet nectar deep inside. Because they can reach into the flower to suck its nectar, they are a favorite of hummingbirds.

The fruit of the Orange Honeysuckle develop as bunches of translucent, orange berries. Coastal Indian children also liked to suck the nectar from the base of the honeysuckle flower.

Pacific Ninebark is an erect to spreading shrub with what is believed to be nine layers of peeling bark. It produces small, white flowers that develop into reddish bunches of fruit. First Nations made knitting needles from the wood.

Red Flowering Currant is a tall, erect shrub. It produces white to red flowers in drooping clusters that indicate the beginning of spring. The flowers, which attract hummingbirds, develop into bluish-black berries that are edible, but not very tasty.

Red Elderberry, or Red Elder, is a tall shrub that can grow to 6 m. It produces clusters of creamy flowers with a strong, unpleasant odor. The flowers develop into bright red fruit. Blue Elderberry, which produces blue fruit, can also be found on Mayne.

Red-Osier Dogwood is a spreading shrub that can grow to 6 m tall. The branches are often bright red in color. It produces small clusters of greenish flowers, which develop into bluish-white fruit. Although the fruit is very bitter, dogwood is a very important source of food for the deer on Mayne.

Salal means *this plentiful shrub*. This is for good reason, as it is probably the most dominant shrub in the Mayne forests. Salal is an upright or ground crawling plant that can grow sparsely or form a dense barrier that is almost impossible to penetrate. It spreads by suckering layer upon layer.

Salal produces pink flowers that give way to bluish-black berries. The berries, which are juicy, sweet and aromatic, make excellent jams, jellies and wine.

Salmonberry is a branching shrub that often forms dense thickets. It produces pink, red or purple flowers. The flowers develop into mushy, edible, yellow or salmon colored berries. The berries of the Salmonberry are one of the earliest berries to ripen in the spring.

Scotch Broom is a bushy shrub with long, thin stems from which sprout yellow flowers in the spring and pea-shaped pods in the summer.

Around the time that the gold miners were stopping at Miners Bay, a

European sea captain was immigrating to Vancouver Island. He brought with him some Scotch Broom seeds that he had picked up from the Hawaiian Islands. Like Gorse, broom can remove the nitrogen it needs from the air, so when the first white settlers began to arrive, it quickly invaded Mayne and the other Gulf Islands.[220]

Today, Scotch Broom grows in abundance on Mayne, particularly on Felix Jack Road. It produces a toxin that can depress the heart and nervous system. It is also a fire hazard.

Sitka Alder is a tall shrub that can grow to 5 m. It produces a spike-like flower cluster. It also produces clusters of cones from which tiny nuts can be shaken.

Sitka Mountain Ash is an erect shrub that produces small, white clusters of flowers. Its red, berry-like fruits are edible, but very bitter.

Stink Currant is an erect shrub with a skunky smell. It produces greenish clusters of flowers that develop into long clusters of edible, bluish-black berries.

Soopolallie, also called Soapberry or Canadian Buffalo-Berry, is a spreading shrub with branches that are covered with scabs. It produces yellowish-brown flowers. Its bright red berries, which feel soapy to the touch, were used by First Nations to make ice cream.

Sword-Fern, also known as the Pala-Pala plant, is one of the most abundant of the ferns found on Mayne. It is often found growing, along with Western Red Cedar, in damp shady forests. Deer Fern, which resembles the Sword-Fern, also grows on Mayne. A good place to see both ferns is in Mount Parke Regional Park.

White-Flowered Rhododendron is a slender, erect shrub with peeling bark. It produces clusters of creamy, cup-shaped flowers. Rhododendron is often found along with the False Azalea and Copperbush plants.

Credits

Historical Photos

British Columbia Archives and Records Services

Royal British Columbia Museum

Salt Spring Archives

Mayne Island Volunteer Firefighters Association

British Columbia Ferry Services Archives

Current Photos

Dreamstime™
Tony Campbell, David Coleman, Galina Barskaya, Paul Wolf, Scott Pehrson, Marilyn Barbone, Steffen Foerster, Steve Degenhardt, Melissa King

Georgia Strait Alliance
Orca Pass International Stewardship Area

Joanie McCorry
Mayne Island Quilters Guild

Darrel Perfumo
En-Vision Gallery

Brian Haller
Santa Ship, Bonfire in Miners Bay Community Park, Easter Egg Hunt

Efraim Gavrilovich
Japanese Garden lights

Credits

Acknowledgements

The Gulf Islanders: Sound Heritage, Volume V, Number 4

Island Heritage Buildings – Thomas K. Ovanin, Islands Trust

A Gulf Islands Patchwork: Some Early Events on the Islands of Galiano, Mayne, Saturna, North and South Pender – British Columbia Historical Association

More Tales from the Outer Gulf Islands: An Anthology of Memories and Anecdotes – British Columbia Historical Association

Mayne Island & The Outer Gulf Islands: A History – Marie Elliott

Mayne Island Post Office: 100th Anniversary – Canada Post

Plumper Pass Lockup and Mayne Island Museum – Mayne Island Agricultural Society

Mayne Island School Centennial: 1883-1983 – Mayne Island School Centenary Committee

Mayne Island Fall Fair: Centennial Year – Mayne Island Agriculture Society

MayneLiner Magazine – ALEA Design & Print

The Terror Of The Coast: Land Alienation And Colonial War On Vancouver Island And The Gulf Islands – Chris Arnett

Vanishing British Columbia – Michael Kluckner

The Gulf Islands Explorer: The Complete Guide – Bruce Obee

Exploring the Best of the Southern Gulf Islands & Sidney: Premier Issue 2005

Hiking the Gulf Islands: An Outdoor Guide to BC's Enchanted Isles – Charles Kahn

Plants of the Pacific Northwest Coast – Pojar and Mackinnon

Birds of the Pacific Northwest Coast – Nancy Baron & John Acorn

Mammals of the Northwest: Washington, Oregon, Idaho and British Columbia – Earl J. Larrison

The Beachcomber's Guide to Seashore Life in the Pacific Northwest – J. Duane Sept

A Year on the Wild Side: - Briony Penn

WetCoast Words: A Dictionary of British Columbia Words and Phrases – Tom Parkin

THe AuthoR

Vicky Lindholm moved with her husband to Mayne Island, in December of 2004. Having authored over 30 pieces of computer courseware, she brought with her more than 20 years of writing experience.

Mayne Island: Facts And Folklore is the first book of its kind to be written by this author, who reviewed over 50 existing pieces of literature and explored parks, beaches and wildlife in order to produce this historical view of Mayne Island. The book is an historical guide to Mayne Island's events, landmarks, parks, beaches, shops, restaurants and wildlife. It includes over 200 photos, past to present, most of which the author photographed herself.

Vicky currently lives and works on Mayne Island. In addition to making a living as a writer, she manages a small gift store, as a home-based business, from her residential property.

INdeX

Notes

[1] **Four Years in British Columbia and Vancouver:** An Account of their Forests, Rivers, Coasts, Gold Fields and Resources for Colonisation – Commander R.C. Mayne, R.N., F.R.G.S., pp. 46 & 355

[2] **The Cariboo Gold Rush Story** – Don Waite, pp 23

[3] **Mayne Island Fall Fair:** Centennial Year – Mayne Island Agriculture Society, pp. 27 and **Barkerville Gold Rush website**

[4] **BC place name cards**, or correspondence between British Columbia's Chief Geographer or the Geographical Names Office – Government of British Columbia

[5] **Mayne Island & The Outer Gulf Islands:** A History – Marie Elliott, pp. 32

[6] **Mayne Island & The Outer Gulf Islands:** A History – Marie Elliott, pp. 127

[7] **Mayne Island & The Outer Gulf Islands:** A History – Marie Elliott, pp. 127

[8] **Mayne Island Fall Fair:** Centennial Year – Mayne Island Agriculture Society, pp. 27

[9] **Mayne Island Fall Fair:** Centennial Year – Mayne Island Agriculture Society, pp. 27

[10] **Mayne Island Post Office:** 100th Anniversary – Canada Post, pp. 1

[11] **Mayne Island Fall Fair:** Centennial Year – Mayne Island Agriculture Society, pp. 27 and inside cover

[12] **Winifred Grey:** A Gentlewoman's Remembrances of Life in England and the Gulf Islands of British Columbia 1871-1910 – Winifred Grey, pp. 125

[13] **BC place name cards**, or correspondence between British Columbia's Chief Geographer or the Geographical Names Office – Government of British Columbia

[14] **Four Years in British Columbia and Vancouver:** An Account of their Forests, Rivers, Coasts, Gold Fields and Resources for Colonisation – Commander R.C. Mayne, R.N., F.R.G.S., pp. 46 & 355

[15] **Mayne Island & The Outer Gulf Islands**: A History – Marie Elliott, pp. 4

[16] **Mayne Island & The Outer Gulf Islands**: A History – Marie Elliott, pp. 13

[17] **Mayne Island & The Outer Gulf Islands**: A History – Marie Elliott, pp. 4

[18] **Mayne Island & The Outer Gulf Islands**: A History – Marie Elliott, pp. 15

[19] **Mayne Island & The Outer Gulf Islands**: A History – Marie Elliott, pp. 63

[20] **MayneLiner Magazine:** Volume 15, Number 8, pp. 49

[21] **Mayne Island Post Office**: 100th Anniversary – Canada Post, pp. 2

[22] **Mayne Island Post Office**: 100th Anniversary – Canada Post, pp. 1

[23] **Mayne Island Fall Fair**: Centennial Year - Mayne Island Agriculture Society, pp. 27

[24] **Mayne Island Post Office**: 100th Anniversary – Canada Post, pp. 3

[25] **Mayne Island Fall Fair**: Centennial Year - Mayne Island Agriculture Society, pp. 23

[26] **A Gulf Islands Patchwork**: Some Early Events on the Islands of Galiano, Mayne, Saturna, North and South Pender – British Columbia Historical Association, pp. 131

[27] **Mayne Island Post Office**: 100th Anniversary – Canada Post, pp. 4

[28] **A Gulf Islands Patchwork**: Some Early Events on the Islands of Galiano, Mayne, Saturna, North and South Pender – British Columbia Historical Association, pp. 170

[29] **Mayne Island Post Office**: 100th Anniversary – Canada Post, pp. 3
[30] **Mayne Island Fall Fair**: Centennial Year - Mayne Island Agriculture Society, pp. 23
[31] **Island Heritage Buildings** – Thomas K. Ovanin, Islands Trust, pp. 108
[32] **Mayne Island Post Office**: 100th Anniversary – Canada Post, pp. 3
[33] **Mayne Island Fall Fair**: Centennial Year - Mayne Island Agriculture Society, pp. 24
[34] **Island Heritage Buildings** – Thomas K. Ovanin, Islands Trust, pp. 108
[35] **Plumper Pass Lockup and Mayne Island Museum** – Mayne Island Agricultural Society, pp. 1
[36] **Plumper Pass Lockup and Mayne Island Museum** – Mayne Island Agricultural Society, pp. 7
[37] **Plumper Pass Lockup and Mayne Island Museum** – Mayne Island Agricultural Society, pp. 7
[38] **Plumper Pass Lockup and Mayne Island Museum** – Mayne Island Agricultural Society, pp. 6
[39] **The Gulf Islands Explorer**: The Complete Guide – Bruce Obee, pp. 166
[40] **Plumper Pass Lockup and Mayne Island Museum** – Mayne Island Agricultural Society, pp. 8
[41] **A Gulf Islands Patchwork**: Some Early Events on the Islands of Galiano, Mayne, Saturna, North and South Pender – British Columbia Historical Association, pp. 28
[42] **Royal Canadian Mounted Police website** – Historical Highlights
[43] **Islands Trust website**
[44] **Mayne Island Fall Fair**: Centennial Year - Mayne Island Agriculture Society, pp. 10 & 32
[45] **Mayne Island Fall Fair**: Centennial Year - Mayne Island Agriculture Society, pp. 10
[46] **Mayne Island & The outer Gulf Islands**: A History – Marie Elliott, pp. 55
[47] **More Tales from the Outer Gulf Islands:** An Anthology of Memories and Anecdotes – British Columbia Historical Association, pp. 150
[48] **Mayne Island & The outer Gulf Islands**: A History – Marie Elliott, pp. 59
[49] **Mayne Island Fall Fair**: Centennial Year - Mayne Island Agriculture Society, pp. 8
[50] **Mayne Island & The Outer Gulf Islands:** A History – Marie Elliott, pp. 62
[51] **More Tales from the Outer Gulf Islands:** An Anthology of Memories and Anecdotes – British Columbia Historical Association, pp. 273
[52] **More Tales from the Outer Gulf Islands:** An Anthology of Memories and Anecdotes – British Columbia Historical Association, pp. 171 & 218
[53] **Mayne Island Fall Fair:** Centennial Year – Mayne Island Agriculture Society, pp. 25
[54] **Mayne Island Fall Fair:** Centennial Year – Mayne Island Agriculture Society, pp. 24
[55] **More Tales from the Outer Gulf Islands:** An Anthology of Memories and Anecdotes – British Columbia Historical Association, pp. 169
[56] **Mayne Island & The Outer Gulf Islands**: A History – Marie Elliott, pp. 37
[57] **Mayne Island & The Outer Gulf Islands**: A History – Marie Elliott, pp. 37
[58] **Mayne Island Chamber of Commerce** – Alan Cheek

[59] **Mayne Island & The Outer Gulf Islands**: A History – Marie Elliott, pp. 37
[60] **Vanishing British Columbia** – Michael Kluckner, pp. 150
[61] **A Gulf Islands Patchwork**: Some Early Events on the Islands of Galiano, Mayne, Saturna, North and South Pender – British Columbia Historical Association, pp. 176
[62] **Vanishing British Columbia** – Michael Kluckner, pp. 150
[63] **Mayne Island & The outer Gulf Islands**: A History – Marie Elliott, pp. 68
[64] **The Georgia Strait Chronicles** – Terry Glavin
[65] **Vanishing British Columbia** – Michael Kluckner, pp. 151
[66] **More Tales from the outer Gulf Islands:** An Anthology of Memories and Anecdotes – British Columbia Historical Association, pp. 164
[67] **Mayne Island & The Outer Gulf Islands:** A History – Marie Elliott, pp. 32
[68] **Mayne Island School Centennial:** 1883-1983 – Mayne Island School Centenary Committee, pp. 1
[69] **Mayne Island School Centennial**: 1883-1983 – Mayne Island School Centenary Committee, pp. 1
[70] **Mayne Island & The Outer Gulf Islands**: A History – Marie Elliott, pp. 15
[71] **Mayne Island School Centennial**: 1883-1983 – Mayne Island School Centenary Committee, pp. 2
[72] **Mayne Island School Centennial**: 1883-1983 – Mayne Island School Centenary Committee, pp. 11
[73] **Mayne Island School Centennial**: 1883-1983 – Mayne Island School Centenary Committee, pp. 3
[74] **Mayne Island School Centennial**: 1883-1983 – Mayne Island School Centenary Committee, pp. 4
[75] **Mayne Island School Centennial**: 1883-1983 – Mayne Island School Centenary Committee, pp. 4
[76] **Mayne Island Fall Fair**: Centennial Year - Mayne Island Agriculture Society, pp. 8
[77] **Mayne Island Fall Fair**: Centennial Year - Mayne Island Agriculture Society, pp. 8
[78] **Mayne Island Fall Fair:** Centennial Year – Mayne Island Agriculture Society, pp. 8
[79] **Mayne Island Fall Fair**: Centennial Year - Mayne Island Agriculture Society, pp. 8
[80] **Mayne Island & The outer Gulf Islands**: A History – Marie Elliott, pp. 29
[81] **Mayne Island & The Outer Gulf Islands:** A History – Marie Elliott, pp. 54
[82] **Mayne Island Fall Fair:** Centennial Year – Mayne Island Agriculture Society, inside cover
[83] **Mayne Island Fall Fair:** Centennial Year – Mayne Island Agriculture Society, inside cover
[84] **Mayne Island & The Outer Gulf Islands:** A History – Marie Elliott, pp. 114
[85] **Mayne Island & The Outer Gulf Islands:** A History – Marie Elliott, pp. 114
[86] **Office Community Plan No. 86, 1994** – Mayne Island Local Trust Committee
[87] **A Gulf Islands Patchwork**: Some Early Events on the Islands of Galiano, Mayne, Saturna, North and South Pender – British Columbia Historical Association, pp. 1

[88] **The Terror Of The Coast**: Land Alienation And Colonial War On Vancouver Island And The Gulf Islands – Chris Arnett, pp. 126

[89] **The Yinka Déné Language Institute website**: The First Nations Languages of British Columbia, Chinook Jargon

[90] **The Terror Of The Coast:** Land Alienation And Colonial War On Vancouver Island And The Gulf Islands – Chris Arnett, pp. 31 & 317

[91] **The Terror Of The Coast:** Land Alienation And Colonial War On Vancouver Island And The Gulf Islands – Chris Arnett, pp. 112

[92] **The Terror Of The Coast**: Land Alienation And Colonial War On Vancouver Island And The Gulf Islands – Chris Arnett, pp. 112

[93] **The Terror Of The Coast:** Land Alienation And Colonial War On Vancouver Island And The Gulf Islands – Chris Arnett, pp. 112

[94] **The Terror Of The Coast:** Land Alienation And Colonial War On Vancouver Island And The Gulf Islands – Chris Arnett, pp. 128

[95] **The Terror Of The Coast:** Land Alienation And Colonial War On Vancouver Island And The Gulf Islands – Chris Arnett, pp. 131 & 132

[96] **The Terror Of The Coast:** Land Alienation And Colonial War On Vancouver Island And The Gulf Islands – Chris Arnett, pp. 132 & 135

[97] **The Terror Of The Coast:** Land Alienation And Colonial War On Vancouver Island And The Gulf Islands – Chris Arnett, pp. 139

[98] **The Terror Of The Coast:** Land Alienation And Colonial War On Vancouver Island And The Gulf Islands – Chris Arnett, pp. 157, 202, 235, 247 & back cover

[99] **The Terror Of The Coast:** Land Alienation And Colonial War On Vancouver Island And The Gulf Islands – Chris Arnett, pp. 140, 184,254, 304 & 308

[100] **More Tales from the Outer Gulf Islands:** An Anthology of Memories and Anecdotes – British Columbia Historical Association, pp. 149

[101] **The Terror Of The Coast:** Land Alienation And Colonial War On Vancouver Island And The Gulf Islands – Chris Arnett, pp. 13

[102] **The Terror Of The Coast**: Land Alienation And Colonial War On Vancouver Island And The Gulf Islands – Chris Arnett, pp. 308

[103] **Indian and Northern Affairs Canada**: The View From The Ferry – Gabriele Helmig

[104] **British Columbia First Nation website**: Band Profiles, Tsartlip Band

[105] **Indian and Northern Affairs Canada**: The View From The Ferry – Gabriele Helmig

[106] **Indian and Northern Affairs Canada**: The View From The Ferry – Gabriele Helmig

[107] **Southern Gulf Islands**: An Altitude SuperGuide – Spalding, Montgomery and Pitt, pp. 61

[108] **Mayne Island Chamber of Commerce website**

[109] **Mayne Island & The Outer Gulf Islands**: A History – Marie Elliott, pp. 34

[110] **Mayne Island & The Outer Gulf Islands**: A History – Marie Elliott, pp. 47

[111] **Mayne Island Fall Fair**: Centennial Year - Mayne Island Agriculture Society, pp. 6

[112] **Mayne Island & The Outer Gulf Islands**: A History – Marie Elliott, pp. 105

[113] **Island Heritage Buildings** – Thomas K. Ovanin, Islands Trust, pp. 107

[114] **Mayne Island Fall Fair:** Centennial Year – Mayne Island Agriculture Society, pp. 27

[115] **Vanishing British Columbia** – Michael Kluckner, pp. 149

[116] **Island Heritage Buildings** – Thomas K. Ovanin, Islands Trust, pp. 107

[117] **Springwater Lodge website**

[118] **Mayne Island & The Outer Gulf Islands**: A History – Marie Elliott, pp. 33 & 34

[119] **Mayne Island & The Outer Gulf Islands**: A History – Marie Elliott, pp. 49

[120] **The Tinkerer's website**

[121] **Mayne Island & The Outer Gulf Islands**: A History – Marie Elliott, pp. 14

[122] **Galiano Museum and Archives**: The Georgeson Collection – Salt Spring Archives

[123] **A Gulf Islands Patchwork**: Some Early Events on the Islands of Galiano, Mayne, Saturna, North and South Pender – British Columbia Historical Association, pp. 45

[124] **BC place name cards**, or correspondence between British Columbia's Chief Geographer or the Geographical Names Office – Government of British Columbia

[125] **Mayne Island Fall Fair**: Centennial Year - Mayne Island Agriculture Society, pp. 21

[126] **BC place name cards**, or correspondence between British Columbia's Chief Geographer or the Geographical Names Office – Government of British Columbia

[127] **Mayne Island Fall Fair**: Centennial Year – Mayne Island Agriculture Society, pp. 21

[128] **The Gulf Islanders**: Sound Heritage, Volume V, Number 4, pp. 64-68

[129] **Mayne Island Fall Fair**: Centennial Year – Mayne Island Agriculture Society, pp. 21

[130] **Mayne Island Fall Fair**: Centennial Year – Mayne Island Agriculture Society, pp. 21

[131] **BC place name cards**, or correspondence between British Columbia's Chief Geographer or the Geographical Names Office – Government of British Columbia

[132] **Mayne Island Fall Fair**: Centennial Year – Mayne Island Agriculture Society, pp. 21

[133] **Southern Gulf Islands**: An Altitude SuperGuide – Spalding, Montgomery and Pitt, pp. 68

[134] **The Gulf Islands Explorer:** The Complete Guide – Bruce Obee, pp. 168

[135] **Mayne Island & The Outer Gulf Islands**: A History – Marie Elliott, pp. 44

[136] **Mayne Island Fall Fair**: Centennial Year - Mayne Island Agriculture Society, pp. 11

[137] **Mayne Island Fall Fair**: Centennial Year - Mayne Island Agriculture Society, pp. 11

[138] **A Gulf Islands Patchwork**: Some Early Events on the Islands of Galiano, Mayne, Saturna, North and South Pender – British Columbia Historical Association, pp. 27

[139] **Mayne Island Fall Fair**: Centennial Year - Mayne Island Agriculture Society, pp. 11

[140] **Mayne Island Fall Fair:** Centennial Year – Mayne Island Agriculture Society, pp. 11

[141] **Island Heritage Buildings** – Thomas K. Ovanin, Islands Trust, pp. 110

[142] **A Gulf Islands Patchwork**: Some Early Events on the Islands of Galiano, Mayne, Saturna, North and South Pender – British Columbia Historical Association, pp. 47

[143] **A Gulf Islands Patchwork**: Some Early Events on the Islands of Galiano, Mayne, Saturna, North and South Pender – British Columbia Historical Association, pp. 94

[144] **Mayne Island Fall Fair**: Centennial Year - Mayne Island Agriculture Society, pp. 34

[145] **St. Mary Magdalene Anglican Church website**

[146] **Meadowmist Farm website**

[147] **A Gulf Islands Patchwork**: Some Early Events on the Islands of Galiano, Mayne, Saturna, North and South Pender – British Columbia Historical Association, pp. 10

[148] **A Gulf Islands Patchwork**: Some Early Events on the Islands of Galiano, Mayne, Saturna, North and South Pender – British Columbia Historical Association, pp. 10

[149] **A Gulf Islands Patchwork:** Some Early Events on the Islands of Galiano, Mayne, Saturna, North and South Pender – British Columbia Historical Association, pp. 10

[150] **Mayne Island School Centennial**: 1883-1983 – Mayne Island School Centenary Committee, pp. 2

[151] **A Gulf Islands Patchwork**: Some Early Events on the Islands of Galiano, Mayne, Saturna, North and South Pender – British Columbia Historical Association, pp. 12

[152] **Mayne Island Fall Fair**: Centennial Year - Mayne Island Agriculture Society, pp. 7

[153] **A Gulf Islands Patchwork**: Some Early Events on the Islands of Galiano, Mayne, Saturna, North and South Pender – British Columbia Historical Association, pp. 12

[154] **Mayne Island & The Outer Gulf Islands**: A History – Marie Elliott, pp. 34

[155] **Vanishing British Columbia** – Michael Kluckner, pp. 150

[156] **Mayne Island Fall Fair**: Centennial Year - Mayne Island Agriculture Society, pp. 23

[157] **Vanishing British Columbia** – Michael Kluckner, pp. 150

[158] **Vanishing British Columbia** – Michael Kluckner, pp. 150

[159] **Island Heritage Buildings** – Thomas K. Ovanin, Islands Trust, pp. 106

[160] **Four Years in British Columbia and Vancouver:** An Account of their Forests, Rivers, Coasts, Gold Fields and Resources for Colonisation – Commander R.C. Mayne, R.N., F.R.G.S., pp. 12

[161] **Mayne Island Post Office**: 100th Anniversary – Canada Post, pp. 3

[162] **Island Tides Newspaper:** Volume 17, Number 15, pp. 4

[163] **Island Tides Newspaper:** Volume 17, Number 15, pp. 4

[164] **MayneLiner Magazine:** Volume 13, Number 11, pp. 55

[165] **Mayne Island Volunteer Firefighter's Association website**

[166] **Mayne Island Fall Fair**: Centennial Year - Mayne Island Agriculture Society, pp. 10

[167] **Mayne Island & The Outer Gulf Islands**: A History – Marie Elliott, pp. 55

[168] **Valhalla Gardens website**

[169] **MayneLiner Magazine:** Volume 15, Number 7, pp. 29

[170] **MayneLiner Magazine:** Volume 15, Number 7, pp. 30

[171] **MayneLiner Magazine:** Volume 15, Number 7, pp. 29

[172] **MayneLiner Magazine:** Volume 15, Number 7, pp. 31

[173] **PerfectCustomers websites:** Mayne Island Quilters Go International

[174] **Island Tides Newspaper:** Volume 16, Number 15, pp. 7

[175] **Island Tides Newspaper:** Volume 16, Number 15, pp. 7

[176] **Mayne Island Fall Fair**: Centennial Year - Mayne Island Agriculture Society, pp. 32

[177] **Passage Ways Newsletter:** Point Roberts Marina Resort, David Zaharik

[178] **Passage Ways Newsletter:** Point Roberts Marina Resort, David Zaharik

[179] **Gulf Islands National Park Reserve of Canada website**: Pacific Marine Heritage Legacy, Parks Canada

[180] **Gulf Islands National Park Reserve of Canada website**: Visitor Information, Parks Canada

[181] **BC place name cards**, or correspondence between British Columbia's Chief Geographer or the Geographical Names Office – Government of British Columbia

[182] **Transportation Safety Board of Canada**: Air 1999

[183] **More Tales from the Outer Gulf Islands:** An Anthology of Memories and Anecdotes – British Columbia Historical Association, pp. 145

[184] **Mayne Island Chamber of Commerce website**

[185] **Four Years in British Columbia and Vancouver:** An Account of their Forests, Rivers, Coasts, Gold Fields and Resources for Colonisation – Commander R.C. Mayne, R.N., F.R.G.S., pp. 6-8 & 80

[186] **Mayne Island & The Outer Gulf Islands**: A History – Marie Elliott, pp. 127

[187] **Mayne Island Fall Fair:** Centennial Year – Mayne Island Agriculture Society, pp. 12

[188] **Mayne Island & The Outer Gulf Islands**: A History – Marie Elliott, pp. 43

[189] **More Tales from the Outer Gulf Islands:** An Anthology of Memories and Anecdotes – British Columbia Historical Association, pp. 159

[190] **Mayne Island Fall Fair**: Centennial Year - Mayne Island Agriculture Society, pp. 36

[191] **The Gulf Islands Explorer**: The Complete Guide – Bruce Obee, pp. 170

[192] **The Georgia Strait Chronicles** – Terry Glavin

[193] **Vanishing British Columbia** – Michael Kluckner, pp. 151

[194] **A Gulf Islands Patchwork**: Some Early Events on the Islands of Galiano, Mayne, Saturna, North and South Pender – British Columbia Historical Association, pp. 176

[195] **Vanishing British Columbia** – Michael Kluckner, pp. 151

[196] **Mayne Island & The Outer Gulf Islands**: A History – Marie Elliott, pp. 54

[197] **The Gulf Islanders:** Sound Heritage, Volume V, Number 4, pp. 49

[198] **Mayne Island Fall Fair:** Centennial Year – Mayne Island Agriculture Society, inside cover

[199] **Mayne Island Fall Fair:** Centennial Year – Mayne Island Agriculture Society, back cover

[200] **Mayne Island & The Outer Gulf Islands**: A History – Marie Elliott, pp. 54

[201] **Mayne Island & The Outer Gulf Islands**: A History – Marie Elliott, pp. 17

[202] **Mayne Island & The Outer Gulf Islands**: A History – Marie Elliott, pp. 17

[203] **The Gulf Islanders:** Sound Heritage, Volume V, Number 4, pp. 5 & 43

[204] **A Gulf Islands Patchwork**: Some Early Events on the Islands of Galiano, Mayne, Saturna, North and South Pender – British Columbia Historical Association, pp. 29

[205] **Coast Salish Villages of Puget Sound website:** Lummi-Bellingham section

[206] **A Gulf Islands Patchwork**: Some Early Events on the Islands of Galiano, Mayne, Saturna, North and South Pender – British Columbia Historical Association, pp. 13

[207] **Mayne Island Fall Fair**: Centennial Year - Mayne Island Agriculture Society, pp. 25

[208] **Mayne Island Post Office**: 100th Anniversary – Canada Post, pp. 3 & 6

[209] **Mayne Island & The Outer Gulf Islands**: A History – Marie Elliott, pp. 49

[210] **Mayne Island & The Outer Gulf Islands**: A History – Marie Elliott, pp. 89

[211] **Mayne Island Fall Fair**: Centennial Year - Mayne Island Agriculture Society, pp. 23

[212] **Mayne Island & The Outer Gulf Islands**: A History – Marie Elliott, pp. 96

[213] **Mayne Island & The Outer Gulf Islands**: A History – Marie Elliott, pp. 115

[214] **Galiano Museum and Archives**: The Georgeson Collection, Interview with Joan Carolan – Salt Spring Archives

[215] **A Year on the Wild Side** – Briony Penn, pp. 76-78

[216] **Mayne Island Fall Fair:** Centennial Year – Mayne Island Agriculture Society, pp. 16

[217] **Gulf Islands National Park Reserve of Canada**: Visitor Guide – Parks Canada, pp. 15

[218] **City of Placerville, California website**

[219] **Plants of the Pacific Northwest Coast:** Washington, Oregon, British Columbia and Alaska

[220] **Plants of the Pacific Northwest Coast:** Washington, Oregon, British Columbia and Alaska